MIME

MINDSET   I'M POSSIBLE   MEDIOCRITY   EXTROARDINARY

Heather Williams

TABLE OF CONTENTS

Prelude: From Ordinary to Extraordinary

When most people hear the word "mime," they think of a performer — silent, deliberate, expressing an entire world without speaking a single word. My life has, in many ways, been its own form of mime. Not in paint or stripes, but in the way I've have moved, adapted, and expressed myself through action rather than noise.

This book, *M·I·M·E*, is about discovering and owning your voice— even when that voice isn't spoken aloud. It's about realizing that true expression is not limited to the sound of words but is found in the quiet strength of your actions, the deliberate movements you make toward your goals, and the everyday choices that reflect who you are at your core. It's about the subtle but powerful mindset shifts that change the course of your life, often without fanfare or applause. In these pages, you'll see how influence can be felt in the way you lead, the way you rise after setbacks, and the way you keep showing up when it would be easier to fade into the background.

Sometimes, the most profound statements you'll ever make are written not with ink or sound, but with the way you live your life— speaking volumes without uttering a single word.

I began my career at McDonald's. It wasn't glamorous, and it wasn't the kind of place most people envision as a launch pad to a thriving future. But for me, it was the ultimate training ground. Behind the counter and under the golden arches, I learned the discipline to show up—on time, every time—ready to perform. I mastered the art of moving at a relentless pace while keeping a smile on my face, even when the line wrapped around the building. I discovered how to lead and connect with people from all walks of life, a skill that would later become the backbone of my success.

McDonald's taught me to manage chaos without losing my cool, to deliver results under pressure, and to spot potential where others saw limitations. And I'm in good company—many well-known figures started their careers in those same uniforms, from comedian Jay Leno to golf legend Tiger Woods, and even Amazon founder Jeff Bezos. They, like me, learned early that the job wasn't just about flipping burgers—it was about building resilience, adaptability, and grit.

We all must start somewhere, and I can say with certainty that I started in the right place. McDonald's gave me more than a paycheck; it gave me the foundation to become the best version of myself. It shaped my work ethic, sharpened my leadership instincts, and instilled in me the drive to keep growing long after I hung up the headset. What began as an entry-level job became the first steppingstone toward an extraordinary career.

When I transitioned into healthcare— specifically into call center operations—it was unexpected. People doubted that someone from fast food could manage a high-stakes environment dealing with patient care, insurance navigation, and complex regulatory systems. But that doubt became fuel. Every leadership position I've held since has been proof that your past is relevant to your future—it's the mindset that matters.

Opportunities came even when I didn't expect them, and I learned quickly that growth never stops. Healthcare is an ever-changing landscape, and my McDonald's foundation gave me the structure and discipline to adapt. In healthcare, adaptability isn't optional—it's essential. Processes evolve, regulations shift, and technology advances, all in the name of delivering better care.

I realized that critical thinking in this field isn't just a nice skill to have—it's the lifeline of the work we do. Every decision carry weight because it directly impacts people's well-being. Discovering solutions, anticipating challenges, and staying calm under pressure became second nature. My years of managing chaos at McDonald's translated seamlessly into navigating complex patient service systems. The pace was different, the stakes higher, but the principles remained the same:

lead with clarity, act with purpose, and never stop learning.

In *M·I·M·E*, we break down four pillars:

- **Mindset**

- **I'm Possible**

- **Mediocrity**

- **Extraordinary**

They form the foundation of my journey, and the lessons I hope will empower yours.

Empowerment isn't just a nice-to-have— it's a survival skill in a world that moves faster and changes more rapidly than ever before. To make it, you must learn to empower yourself, to stand firmly in your own worth, and to believe in your ability to grow beyond your current circumstances.

But here's the truth: empowerment doesn't always start from within. Sometimes, it needs a spark from someone else. It might come from a mentor who believes in you before you believe in yourself. It could be born from a hard truth spoken in love. And sometimes, it arrives quietly, tucked inside the pages of a book—maybe even this one— where you find a story that mirrors your own, reminding you that you're not alone and that your "impossible" can become "I'm possible."

No matter where it comes from, that spark is just the beginning. It's up to you to build on it.

Form your foundation, strengthen it with knowledge, courage, and resilience, and commit to evolving. Empowerment isn't a single moment—it's a daily choice. It's deciding that every setback is a setup for something greater, and every challenge is a chance to grow.

This is not just my story; it's an invitation. A call to those who have been overlooked, underestimated, or told they couldn't do something. It's for the introvert asked to lead, the underdog asked to deliver, and the everyday person who knows they were meant for something more.

By the end of this book, I hope you'll not just hear my voice — but find your own.

Chapter 1 – Mindset

Mindset is the invisible architecture of success—the lens that frames every challenge, the filter that shapes every decision, and the quiet force that decides whether you stall at the first obstacle or press on toward something greater. It isn't mystical or complicated; it's practical and trainable.

Start simple. When you wake up, don't ask, "What can't get done today?" Ask, "What **can** I do today?" Make a short "I can" list: one call you can make, one task you can finish, one promise you can keep to yourself. Then do those. Action creates clarity, and clarity compounds confidence. Over time, the things that felt like "can't" begin to shrink because the momentum from your "I can's moves them within reach—or solves them altogether.

Mindset is a daily choice, not a personality trait. Begin with "I can," do what you can, and let consistency stack in your favor. Your mindset is powerful: when you repeatedly complete the "I can" work, the "what can't" work often gets done almost automatically— because you've built enough progress, skill, and belief to make it possible.

"Say 'I can' with your actions, not just your words. Momentum answers the questions doubt keeps asking." — *Heather Williams*

I learned early on that mindset isn't something you're born with—it's something you build, brick by brick, choice by choice. My own journey began at 19, when I chose to become a General Manager at McDonald's instead of going to college. It felt like a win. I was young, ambitious, and proud to hold a leadership title. The paycheck was strong. The perks were shiny. I had a company car with no insurance bill, no maintenance costs, no registration fees. At that age, it sounded like freedom.

But there's a difference between enjoying something and owning it—between being impressed by the perks and being invested in your future. I worked hard for a car that would never be mine. I wore a title that didn't translate into equity. I had access to nice things, but they were borrowed, not built. The lesson hit me slowly: what looks like a shortcut can be a lease on your life. The "win" that pays today can cost you tomorrow if it doesn't create ownership—skills you control, assets you hold, confidence you've earned.

That realization didn't make me bitter; it made me better. It forced me to redefine my strength. A strong mindset isn't just "work harder." It's "work wiser." It asks: Does this choice build something I actually keep? Am I growing skills that travel with me? Am I building relationships and a reputation that no one can repossess? Titles can be taken back.

Perks can be turned off. But discipline, credibility, and competence—those belong to you.

So, I started stacking different bricks: saying yes to responsibilities that stretched me, not just rewarded me; learning how to lead people, not just manage schedules; saving my wins instead of spending them the same day; treating each day as a chance to own one more piece of my life. Some days that meant doing the unglamorous thing—showing up early, staying late, asking for feedback, documenting processes. Other days it meant saying no to what looked good so I could say yes to what would last.

Saying no is not easy and it's something I'm still learning. I'm traditionally a yes-person. I like to help. I like to be the one people can count on. But I realized that every "yes" has a cost—and sometimes that cost is quality, health, or the goals that actually matter.

People-pleasing feels generous in the moment; over time, it can quietly bankrupt your focus.

I had to retrain myself. Instead of asking, "Can I squeeze this in?" I started asking, "Should I own this?" If the answer wasn't a clear yes, I paused. Taking on more is not always good—especially if you can't execute. In leadership, half-finished is sometimes worse than not started. It wastes time, burns trust, and crowds out what would have moved the needle.

To make it practical, I built a few rules:

- **The Fit–Future–Fuel test.** Does it fit our priorities? Does it build the future we want? Does it give energy (or at least not drain it completely)? If I can't say yes to at least two, it's a no.

- **Yes, if... or no, but...** I don't ghost responsibility; I shape it. "Yes, if we can push this to next week and staff it with X." Or "No, but here's a faster path and the person to lead it."

- **Two Big Rocks per day.** I pick the two outcomes that matter most and protect them from noise. Everything else fits around them—or it doesn't.

In practice, this means fewer heroic saves and more predictable systems. At McDonald's, my early "yes" to everything looked like jumping on the line, fixing schedules, and staying until close because I didn't want to disappoint anyone. It made me feel indispensable, but it made the system fragile. Later, in healthcare operations, I learned to build capacity instead of being capacity. We created clear handoffs, "definition of done" checklists, and a simple dashboard for service levels. Saying no to ad- hoc changes let us say a bigger yes to patient experience and team sanity.

Delegation was another brick. Not "dump it and hope," but real delegation: a clear brief, a deadline, the metric, and the authority to decide. I started asking, "Who should own this to grow?" not "Who can do this fastest?" When I did that, people surprised me. They took pride, solved problems I hadn't seen, and brought me options instead of issues. Saying no to doing it myself was saying yes to developing leaders.

Boundaries also became part of execution. I set "no-meeting afternoons" twice a week so I could do deep work. I stopped replying to every message immediately and started answering in batches. I built a "stop-doing list": tasks that felt important because they were familiar, not because they created value. Every quarter, I looked at my calendar like a budget and cut the vanity spend.

I had to make peace with disappointment. Someone would get frustrated when I said no. A request wouldn't be handled the old way.

That's okay. Leadership isn't about avoiding every bump; it's about creating a road that actually gets you—and your team— somewhere worth going. Respect grows when your yes means something and your no protects the mission.

Here's what changed when my yes got selective: execution got cleaner. Projects finished. Metrics moved. The team knew what mattered. We missed fewer handoffs. I was less exhausted, more present, and more consistent. Saying no didn't make me less helpful; it made me reliably helpful.

If you're a people pleaser like me, try this for 30 days:

- Put your top two priorities on the calendar first.

- For new requests, reply with **Yes, if...**

- or **no, but...** (default to one of those).

- Delegate one thing per week with a clear brief and a definition of done.

- End each week by listing the "bricks" you laid finished outcomes, not hours worked.

I still slip. I still say yes too quickly sometimes. But I've learned that discipline is kinder than overcommitment. A focused "no" today protects the quality of tomorrow's "yes." That's how you build, brick by brick— until what you're building finally belongs to you.

My mindset wasn't as strong as I thought back then—but that didn't stop me from growing. In fact, it's what kept me growing. I learned to trade applause for ownership, instant validation for long-term value, borrowed status for built substance. That shift—brick by brick, choice by choice—turned a young manager with perks into a leader with purpose. And that's the point: you don't inherit mindset; you construct it, until one day you look around and realize the life you're living isn't borrowed anymore—it's yours.

I discovered quickly that a title alone doesn't make you a leader. At McDonald's, my performance wasn't about what I personally accomplished—it lived and died by how well my team performed. I was managing people, but I wasn't truly leading them. Most days felt like triage: replacing employees who called out, borrowing products from another store because we ran out, coaxing the ice cream machine back to life, stocking items the prior shift should've handled. I'd work a full day and leave with nothing truly moved forward. No time to prepare for tomorrow meant tomorrow kept ambushing me. And when tomorrow owns you, you can't get ahead— especially in your prime years when learning and growth should be compounding.

The hard truth: firefighting made me feel useful, but it didn't make the store stronger. Leadership asked a different question—not "How fast can I fix this?" but "How do I build a team and a system, so this doesn't break in the first place?"

I changed my job from chief problem-solver to chief system-builder:

- I shifted from rescuing to **resetting expectations** and coaching to those expectations.

- From doing tasks myself to **designing checklists, routines, and ownership** so the right person did the right task at the right time.

- From measuring effort to **measuring outcomes**: speed of service, waste, customer satisfaction, labor efficiency, and crew readiness.

- From "Who can jump in?" to **"Who should own this, so they grow?"**

From fire drills to playbooks (what I put in place)

- **Pre-shift huddles (7 minutes).** Review forecast, assignments by position, and one focus metric. End with, "What might break today, and who's got it?"

- **Shift Readiness Checklist.** Pars set and verified; critical equipment checks (including the ice cream machine); backup stock staged; contingency plan for callouts.

- **Call-out ladder & bench.** A rotating on-call list, cross-training matrix, and a simple group text template to fill holes fast— without me as the bottleneck.

- **Par levels & reorder points.** We stopped "borrowing" by setting minimums, labeling bins, and auditing nightly. If stock dipped below par, the system alerted—not my panic.

- **SOP cards at the station.** Laminated, step-by-step guides for the top 10 recurring issues, plus a "definition of done" for each closing task.

- **After-Action Reviews (10 minutes).** What went well, what broke, what we'll change by next shift. One concrete process tweak each time—no laundry lists.

- **Protected "Tomorrow Time."** Thirty minutes daily (not negotiable) to plan schedules, coach one person, and remove one friction point. If I lost that time, I "paid it back" the same week.

The result? Fewer surprises, cleaner execution, and a team that didn't need me to hover. I traded adrenaline for reliability—and the store got better because people got better.

Leading vs. Managing (quick distinctions)

- **Focus:** Managing = tasks; Leading = outcomes + people.

- **Time horizon:** Managing = today; Leading = today **and** tomorrow.

- **Power source:** Managing = position; Leading = trust and credibility.

- **Response to problems:** Managing = fix it; Leading = **prevent** it and teach others how.

- **Ownership:** Managing = "I'll handle it;" Leading = "You own it—and I'll coach you."

Practical tips to lead (not just manage)

1. **Define "done."** For every recurring task, write the 3–5 checks that mean it's complete. No ambiguity, no rework.

2. **Coach with a cadence.** One 15- minute coaching conversation per week per key person: one strength, one growth target, one next action.

   Make priorities visible. A simple whiteboard with the week's two focus metrics and the owner for each. What's visible gets real.

3. **Delegate outcomes, not errands.** "Reduce order errors to <1% this week; here's the SOP and authority you need. Report Friday."

4. **Install habit triggers.** Tie tasks to time or events (e.g., "At 2:30 pm, always check pars for dinner rush").

5. **Standardize recovery.** When something breaks, the first step is always the same: stabilize, communicate, log root cause, update the playbook.

6. **Protect 'tomorrow time.'** Put planning and development on the calendar first; let meetings work around **that**, not the other way.

7. **Recognize by behavior.** Praise specific actions that match the standard ("Great pre-shift huddle—clear roles and one focus metric").

8. **Say "No, but…"** Decline non-priority requests while offering a path ("No today, but if we hit our focus metric by Thursday, we'll revisit").

9. **Grow a bench.** Always be training your replacement; that's the fastest way to earn your next role.

"A manager can fix a shift. A leader builds people and systems so the shift can fix itself."— *Heather Williams*

The burnout came fast. I stepped down from my GM role and enrolled in college. Even without the title, I couldn't turn off the reflex to fix things. Wherever I worked, I became the unofficial second GM—the one without the nameplate who still ran huddles, stabilized shifts, and coached new hires while studying between breaks. On paper, each store had one general manager. In practice, there were two: the official one, and me—learning to influence without authority.

At first, my mindset was simple: escape fast food. I enrolled in nursing school and earned my associate's degree in science because the community college in my area offered a pathway to an RN license upon completion. I thought I was changing industries; what I didn't realize was that I was also changing how I thought. Pharmacology exams by day and closing shifts by night forced me to prioritize, communicate clearly, and stay calm under pressure. Triage in a classroom or a restaurant rush isn't the same—but the muscles overlap: assess, decide, act, review.

Somewhere in that grind, I noticed something surprising: McDonald's had already given me a toolkit I didn't fully appreciate. Structure.

Discipline. Standards. The ability to perform when the clock and the crowd are both loud. I used to think I was just flipping burgers faster; in reality, I was learning operations— forecasting demand, scheduling labor, managing inventory, troubleshooting equipment, understanding the customer journey end to end. I had ketchup in my blood, and it wasn't a joke—it was a blueprint.

Hamburger University: Where Operations Became a Language I Could Speak Anywhere

A visit to **Hamburger University** sealed it. I saw that McDonald's wasn't only selling meals; it was **teaching management science at scale**. The language on the walls was simple—**Quality, Service, Cleanliness, Value**—but underneath were systems: clear SOPs, measurable metrics, feedback loops, and a relentless focus on repeatability. That visit reframed my "escape." The goal wasn't to run from what I'd learned, but to **run with it**—to apply it where the stakes were even higher.

Profit & Loss: Reading a Business Like a Book

At HU, P&L literacy wasn't an elective; it was the core. We didn't just memorize terms—we **worked the numbers**:

- **Sales** = **Traffic** × **Average Check**. Grow one or both, on purpose.

- **Prime Cost** = **Cost of Goods Sold (COGS)** + **Labor**. Control these and you control the restaurant.

- **Controllables:** paper, utilities, repairs & maintenance—small leaks that sink big ships if you don't track them weekly.

- **Variance analysis:** compare **actual vs. theoretical** food cost to spot waste, theft, or process drift.

- **Break-even & contribution margin:** understand where profit actually begins and which products push you there faster.

Every week became a disciplined ritual: read the P&L, ask *why*, fix one lever, measure next week. It trained my brain to see a business as a living system—one where **what you measure moves**.

Building Sales: Not Luck—Levers

Sales building wasn't "sell harder." It was design:

- **Menu engineering:** *Stars, Plowhorses, Puzzles, Dogs*—price, place, promote based on margin and demand.

- **Mix management & suggestive selling:** nudge toward high-margin add-ons that delight the guest (not push, **guide**).

- **Throughput:** seconds at drive-thru = dollars in daily sales. Reduce friction and watch revenue rise.

- **Daypart strategies:** breakfast vs. lunch vs. late-night—unique labor, prep, and promo for each.

- **Local store marketing:** partner with schools, sports teams, and community events; turn goodwill into traffic.

- **Forecasting:** last year's week + trend + promo calendar + weather/events = smarter orders and smarter schedules.

HU made "sales" concrete: if we shaved 12 seconds off average window time, we could process X more cars per hour. If we raised the average check by $0.25 with one well-placed suggestion, weekly sales increased. **Small inches compounded.**

Systems Thinking: The Engine Behind the Counter

What looked like common sense was formalized into **operating systems**:

- **SOPs** for everything (opening, closing, prep, temp logs) so quality didn't depend on who showed up.

- **Training ladders** and **certifications** so people knew what "good" looked like—and could teach it.

- **Gemba** mindset: go to the place, watch the flow, fix the friction you can see.

- **PDCA cycles** (Plan–Do–Check–Act): test small, learn fast, standardize what works.

- **Scoreboards** are visible to everyone— service time, accuracy, guest feedback—so improvement became a team sport.

HU taught me to treat excellence like a **repeatable pattern**, not a personality trait.

What I Carried into Healthcare

When I crossed over to healthcare operations, nothing was wasted. The vocabulary changed, but the **logic** didn't:

- **Traffic × Average Check → Access & Yield:** call volume, show rates, clean claim rate, reimbursement yield.

- **Prime Cost → Cost to Serve:** labor per call, rework rate, denial cost, bad- debt prevention.

- **Throughput → Flow:** Average Handle Time balanced with **First-Call Resolution** and accuracy.

- **Menu engineering → Service mix:** prioritize high-impact scenarios (benefits verification, EOB clarity, corrected claims) with scripts that **lower anxiety** and **prevent callbacks**.

- **Gemba & PDCA → Continuous improvement:** listen to calls, find the friction (missing info, clumsy handoffs), fix one lever a week, measure visibly.

- **Scoreboards → Shared ownership:** QA trends, FCR, sentiment, rework— all transparent, all tied to behaviors we could practice in 10-minute huddles.

In both worlds, the heart of the work was the same: **make the right way the easy way**.

Whether it's fries at the right temp or PHI verified the right way, standards protect the guest—or the patient—and they protect the team.

The Moment I Stopped "Escaping"

At HU, I realized I didn't need to shed my past to become who I wanted to be. I needed to **transfer it**. McDonald's had handed me **financial fluency**, **operational discipline**, **sales levers**, and **people systems**. Healthcare needed all of those—plus empathy. The formula became M·I·M·E in motion:

- **Mindset:** See constraints as design prompts.

- **I'm Possible:** Stretch into industries that value transferable systems.

- **Mediocrity (as a stage):** Use plateaus to hardwire fundamentals.

- **Extraordinary:** Do the ordinary with such consistency that it becomes trust.

Hamburger University didn't just teach me how to run a restaurant. It taught me how to **run a system**—to read the numbers, improve the flow, grow the people, and connect daily habits to meaningful outcomes. That knowledge doesn't stay behind the counter. It travels—into call centers, clinics, communities, and anywhere the stakes are high, and the mission is human.

"Learn the P&L, respect the SOP, love the people—and you can take that playbook anywhere." -Heather Williams

I pivoted. I switched to business school, earned a bachelor's degree in business with a minor in marketing, and later completed my

MBA. The coursework gave names to what I'd been doing instinctively: process improvement, capacity planning, cost control, brand promise, customer lifetime value. P&L statements stopped being reports and started becoming stories: where we win, where we leak, and what habits create both.

In parallel, I kept working—and kept "fixing." But my fixing evolved. I wasn't jumping on the line as much; I was building the line to run better. I wrote checklists and trained others to run them. I learned to coach with data— "Here's our drive-thru time trend and your best window performance last week; let's replicate that." I practiced leading sideways, gaining buy-in from peers and supervisors by sharing wins, not just opinions. Influence, I learned, is earned in quiet moments: the extra prep before a rush, the respectful follow-up after feedback, the consistency of showing up the same way on good days and hard ones.

That combination—McDonald's muscle and formal education— became my leadership foundation. It shaped a habit I still carry today: I wake up and ask, "What more can I do?" Over time, "more" got smarter. It stopped meaning extra hours and started meaning extra leverage. More isn't always volume; often, it's design. It's the one system that eliminates five recurring headaches. It's the one conversation that unlocks someone else's best. It's the one boundary that protects tomorrow's progress.

Looking back, the arc is clear. I didn't abandon fast food; I graduated from it. I took the discipline of a rush, the clarity of a checklist, and layered it with strategy, marketing, and organizational behavior.

That's why the burnout didn't break me—it redirected me. I shifted from being a title holder to being a builder. From being a rescuer to being a teacher. From managing minutes to compounding value.

And that "fixer" identity? I still have it—but it's different now. I don't race to put out fires first. I design the floorplan, so fewer fires start. I don't aim to be the hero of the shift; I aim to be the architect of a team that doesn't need a hero. That's the quiet confidence McDonald's gave me, business school refined, and life confirmed: structure is freedom, standards are kindness, and preparation is a love language—for your customers, your team, and your own future.

Most of all, I learned that mindset isn't magic—it's a method. Wake up. Ask, "What more can I do?" Start with what you can control. Build one system. Teach one person. Improve one step. The title may change. The industry may change. But the bricks stack the same way, day after day, until the work you've been borrowing from becomes the life you actually own.

Lessons from the Golden Arches

People often ask how I went from managing a McDonald's to running operations for a healthcare call center. My answer is always the same—it started with mindset.

If you've ever managed a lunch rush short- staffed, you know what pressure feels like. I still remember one Friday when a delivery truck had just unloaded, the stockroom was jammed, the drive-thru wrapped around the building, and we were down two employees. I ran a 60-second huddle, reassigned roles on the fly—the fry cook became the runner, the cashier moved to the headset, and I jumped on the grill. Then I gave the team a single rally point: "One order, one smile, one standard at a time."

In moments like that, I learned a powerful truth: **a leader's mindset in chaos becomes the team's mindset**. If I panicked, they panicked. If I stayed calm, they focused and delivered. I stopped trying to be the fastest pair of hands and started being the steadiest voice in the room. That shift followed me everywhere.

When I transitioned to healthcare operations, the parallels were immediate. The lunch rush became Monday-morning spikes. Ticket times became average handle time. Order accuracy became first-call resolution. The same rules applied:

- **Clarity beats speed.** Clear assignments and one focus metric outperform frantic activity.

- **Roles over heroics.** A well-placed person in the right role beats three people in the wrong one.

- **Systems prevent fires.** Checklists, par levels, escalation paths—these are calm printed on paper.

- **Data is the nervous system.** Live boards (queues, SLAs, abandon rate) tell you where to send help.

I carried simple tools from the grill to the phones: five-minute pre-shift huddles, a cross- training matrix, color-coded thresholds (green/yellow/red), and a "lighthouse script" for updates during surges:

Here's what we know. Here's what we're doing. Who owns what? Next update at __.

That mindset doesn't just move lines; it moves people—from stress to steadiness, from guessing to executing.

"In a rush, your voice is the thermostat. Set it to calm, and the room finds its courage." — *Heather Williams*

Steps to Change (from managing chaos to leading through it)

1. **Set your calm standard.**

   Write a 2-sentence crisis script you'll use every time:

   "Team, we're in yellow. Focus metric is _. Roles are set. I'll update at _." Practice it until it's muscle memory.

2. **Do a 5×5 pre-shift huddle (5 minutes, 5 elements).**

   Forecast today's volume, assign roles, name one focus metric, surface top 2 risks, confirm the comms plan (who escalates, when).

3. **Build a "hot-swap" map.**

   Create a cross-training matrix so you know who can cover what for 60–90 minutes. Post it. Use it. Reward people who add a new skill.

4. **Instrument the work.**

   Make the invisible visible: a whiteboard or dashboard with live queue, target, and status lights (green/yellow/red). Define triggers for help or escalation.

5. **Communicate like a lighthouse.**

   Use the four-part update during spikes: **Know → Do → Owners → Next update.** Keep it short. Repeat it often. Consistency lowers anxiety.

6. **Standardize recovery.**

   When something breaks, follow the same path: stabilize, notify, log root cause, update the SOP/checklist. One tweak per incident—no "everything at once."

7. **Protect "tomorrow time."**

   Block 30 minutes daily to fix one recurring issue, coach one person, and prepare one upcoming surge. Guard it like revenue.

8. **Coach outcomes, not effort.** Delegate with a target (*"Reduce abandons to <3% by noon; you have authority to reassign seats."*), not a task list. Review results, then refine.

9. **Debrief every wave (10 minutes).** What worked? What broke? What changes before the next shift? Capture one concrete change and assign an owner.

10. **Model the mindset you want.** Calm tone, clear direction, generous recognition. Your team will mirror

    what you are under pressure more than what you say.

This week's quick start:

- **Today:** Write your crisis script and 5×5 huddle template.

- **Tomorrow:** Build the hot-swap matrix; train one "second" for your most fragile role.

- **By Friday:** Install a simple live board and run two 10-minute debriefs.

- **By next week:** Convert one recurring issue into a written SOP with a definition of done.

Leaders don't eliminate chaos; they **organize** it. And when you organize it, you teach your team how to win on the busiest day—whether it's a drive-thru line at noon or a call queue on Monday morning.

Mindset in Healthcare

Transitioning into healthcare operations raised the stakes. Instead of orders and fries, we were handling appointments, authorizations, test results, and urgent needs. The pace was still intense—but now accuracy and empathy had equal weight with speed. My mindset shifted from "keep the line moving" to "get every detail right **while** keeping the line moving." I leaned on McDonald's discipline, then layered in clinical precision, confidentiality, and a deeper sense of responsibility.

I adopted a dual mandate:

- **Safety before speed;** never trade accuracy for throughput.
- **Clarity with compassion;** the right answer delivered kindly and clearly.

"Overnight" Wins (small changes, big impact)

1. **Two identifiers every time.** Script: "Before we proceed, can I verify your full name and date of birth?" (No exceptions.)

2. **Closed-loop communication.**

   Read back critical info (meds, dates, times, locations): "Let me read that back…"

3. **Teach-back for understanding.** "Just to be sure I explained it well, what's your next step from here?"

4. **Huddles with one focus metric.**

   5 minutes at shift start; name today's target (e.g., FCR, abandon rate) and owner.

5. **Queue triage + hot swap.** Predefine which agents move where when SLA hits yellow/red.

6. **Standardized notes & templates.** Fewer codes, clearer dispositions, fewer reworks.

7. **Rapid patient acknowledgment.**

   If resolution needs time, send a time- stamped update within 30 minutes.

8. **3 calls, 3 moments of coaching per day.**

   Quick feedback beats monthly reviews.

Great things take time—but **results can start tonight** when you standardize small things and do them the same way, every time.

Action Items (be the change agent)

Today

- Write and post your **Crisis & Calm script**: *"We're in yellow. Focus metric: __. Roles set. Next update at__."*
- Implement **Two-ID** + **Read-back** + **Teach-back** as your non-negotiables.
- Start a **10-minute end-of-day debrief**: what worked, what broke, one change for tomorrow.

This Week

- Build a **hot-swap matrix** (who can cover which queue for 60–90 min).
- Stand up a **live metric board** (SLA, AHT, FCR, abandons, callbacks due).
- Create a **QA rubric (5 items)**: identification, empathy, accuracy, documentation, next-step clarity.
- Launch **reminder cadence** to cut no- shows: 48h + 24h + 2h (with confirm/cancel links).

Next 30–90 Days

- **Crosstrain** 30% of staff.
- Run monthly **After-Action Reviews** and update SOPs (one tweak per incident).
- Track outcomes:

1   Abandons ↓ 3–5 pts in 30 days

2   QA compliance → ≥97%

3   FCR ↑ 5 pts without inflating AHT.

Micro-Scripts (precision + empathy)

- **Verify & reassure:**

  "I can help with that. Before we proceed, may I verify your full name and date of birth? Thank you. I know waiting is stressful—here's what I can do right now…"

- **Read-back:**

  "You're scheduled for Tuesday, Sept 9 at 10:30 AM at our Brandon location. Did I get that right?"

- **Teach-back:**

  "Just so we're aligned, what's the next step you'll take after we hang up?"

- **Expectation set:**

  "I'll update you by 3:00 PM. If you don't hear from me, here's our direct line and my ticket number."

Change Agent Toolkit

- **Standardize safety:** Two-ID, read- back, teach-back, and documented handoffs.

- **Instrument the day:** Visible targets; green/yellow/red thresholds with predefined actions.

- **Coach outcomes:** Delegate with targets ("Abandons <3% by noon") and authority.

- **Protect tomorrow:** 30 minutes daily to fix one recurring issue, prep one surge, coach one person.

- **Model the thermostat:** Calm tone, clear steps, consistent follow-through.

Be patient with the big goals—and impatient with the small habits. Great things take time, but the **first** results can be overnight when you tighten a script, clarify a handoff, and make safety automatic. That's how you become the change agent your team—and your patients— can feel.

The Growth Mindset Advantage

Dr. Carol Dweck's research on growth versus fixed mindsets shows that those who believe abilities can be developed are more willing to embrace challenges and persist after setbacks. That became my professional compass.

When things got tough, I stopped asking,

"Why me?" and started asking, *"What can I learn from this?"* That shift turned setbacks into strategies.

Practical Ways to Strengthen Your Mindset

1. **Morning Mental Rehearsal** – Visualize how you'll handle challenges before your day begins.

2. **Reframe Failure** – Identify one failure from the week and write three lessons it taught you.

3. **Language Audit** – Replace "I can't" with "How can I?" to keep your mind focused on solutions.

4. **Surround Yourself with Growth- Minded People** – Your environment shapes your mindset more than you realize.

Closing Thought

Mindset isn't about pretending everything is fine—it's about choosing the **most useful lens** for what's real. A strong mindset doesn't deny constraints; it **defines your response** to them. As a leader, that choice becomes contagious. Your team reads your tone faster than your emails. If you default to curiosity instead of panic, to solutions instead of blame, they will too.

Whether you're in a fast-food kitchen during a lunch rush or a healthcare center on a high- volume day, the principle holds: **your mindset sets the room's emotional temperature**. It shapes psychological safety (Can we speak up?), performance (Can we stretch?), and resilience (Can we bounce back?).

"Leaders don't just solve problems—they set the atmosphere in which problems get solved." – Heather Williams

What strong leadership mindset looks like in practice?

- **Name reality, then name a path.** "This is hard—and here's our first next step."
- **Model the language of possibility.** Swap "We can't" for "How could we...?"
- **Be calmly transparent.** If you don't know yet, say so—and commit to when you will.
- **Pair standards with care.** High expectations, human delivery.
- **Celebrate learning, not just outcomes.** Progress beats perfection.

Daily reset (60 seconds)

1. **Reframe:** What challenge will I choose to see as a chance to improve?
2. **Refocus:** What one action will move us forward today?
3. **Reflect:** What did we learn yesterday that we'll apply now?

Mindset doesn't eliminate the storm; it **anchors the crew**. Held consistently, it will carry you—and the people you lead—through pressure, through transition, and into performance you can be proud of

Chapter 2 – I'm Possible

A quote often attributed to Audrey Hepburn: *"Nothing is impossible. The word itself says, 'I'm possible.'"*

When I first heard it, I thought it was just clever wordplay—something you'd see printed on a poster in a break room or posted on an inspirational Instagram account. But over time, it became my **survival mantra**. It stopped being a catchphrase and started being a reminder—a constant push to see my obstacles differently.

It wasn't just about blind optimism or pretending life was always sunshine. It was about **defying limits**—the limits others placed on me, and the even more dangerous limits I had quietly placed on myself.

"Impossible is just a word we give to something we haven't figured out how to do yet." - Heather Williams

The shift from "impossible" to "I'm possible" is more than just moving a space between letters—it's a **complete change in vision**. "Impossible" sees a brick wall. "I'm possible" sees the bricks as steps. "Impossible" assumes the finish line can't be reached. "I'm possible" starts walking anyway, trusting that the path will appear.

When you say, "I'm possible," you aren't denying reality—you're deciding to meet it differently. You're saying: *I might not have the answers today, but I am capable of finding them.* You're acknowledging that **your future potential is not limited by your current circumstances.**

For me, "I'm possible" became the filter through which I approached career moves, personal challenges, and even leadership decisions. It reminded me that just because something has never been done—or I've never done it—doesn't mean it's not within my reach.

The truth is, nothing is truly impossible until you stop trying. Once you see yourself as possible, you'll start seeing the world that way, too.

From Impossible to I'm Possible

When I decided to leave McDonald's and move into healthcare, a lot of people doubted me. On the surface, the industries looked worlds apart. But I knew the truth: at their core, both demand operational excellence, customer (patient) experience, problem- solving under pressure, and strong, steady leadership.

I still remember my first healthcare leadership interview. On paper, I wasn't the "perfect" candidate.

I didn't have years of clinical background or a resume full of acronyms. What I did have was twenty-plus years of leading teams through chaos, driving results, and building systems that worked. I walked in with confidence rooted in experience. I didn't pretend to know everything—I promised I would learn everything. That's the heart of *"I'm possible."* You don't have to start as the ideal fit; you must believe you can grow into the role—and then do the work to make that belief real.

Leaving McDonald's was one of the hardest decisions of my life. I spent over two decades there, with most of that time in leadership roles. McDonald's wasn't just a job; it shaped how I think, lead, and solve problems. It taught me to anticipate needs before they were spoken and to execute with speed and precision. That foundation carried me through business school, where I earned all A's—not because the classes were easy, but because the knowledge I'd gained on the job transferred directly to the classroom.

Take statistics, for example—the "weed-out" course many dreads. For me, it felt familiar. I'd been doing statistics for years without calling it that: forecasting sales and labor, planning schedules around peak hours, projecting drive-thru volume by time-of-day and adjusting prep lines to hit service-time targets. Queueing, throughput, variance, forecasting—those weren't just terms in a textbook; they were decisions I made every shift to keep the operation humming.

When I stepped into healthcare operations, that same analytical lens became my advantage. What used to be "cars per hour" became "calls per hour." Service time became average handle time. Abandonment rate and service level replaced drive-thru times and order accuracy, but the discipline behind them was the same: predict demand, staff smartly, streamline processes, coach for quality, and never lose sight of the human on the other side of the interaction. In fast food, the experience ends with a meal. In healthcare, the experience can influence someone's health, their anxiety level, even their willingness to seek care again. The stakes were higher—but the muscle memory of operational leadership translated beautifully.

I approached those first 90 days in healthcare with humility and a plan:

- **Listen and learn:** Shadow frontline agents, schedulers, and nurses. Ask questions without ego.
- **Map the system:** Understand intake, scheduling, authorizations, clinical handoffs, billing—where information flows and where it gets stuck.
- **Find quick wins:** Fix the friction you can see—confusing scripts, clunky handoffs, unclear KPIs—so the team feels momentum.

- **Build trust:** Recognize quiet excellence, share credit publicly, and make it safe to surface problems so we can solve them together.

That's what "I'm possible" looked like in practice: belief, backed by preparation, humility, and relentless action.

The identity shift was real. I was leaving a place where I could solve problems in my sleep and stepping into a new world with new acronyms, new regulations, and new consequences. But every time doubt whispered, *"You've never done this,"* I answered, *"I've done what it takes."* My past wasn't an anchor—it was a launchpad. The discipline, speed, and people leadership I'd focus on in one arena simply found new expressions in another.

In the end, the industry change taught me something bigger than a new set of metrics: **growth is portable**. The mindset that helped me move a drive-thru line faster helped me improve patient scheduling. The coaching skills I used to turn crews into teams helped me develop agents into advocates. The operational instincts that trimmed waste and boosted margins helped us reduce wait times and raise satisfaction. The context changed. The core didn't.

"I'm possible" isn't a slogan. It's a strategy. It means you can honor where you came from while refusing to be limited by it. It means you treat every new challenge as a classroom and every doubt as an invitation to prepare better. It means you look at a closed door and ask, *"Where's the other entrance?"*

I didn't jump industries because I had all the answers. I jumped because I trusted my capacity to learn, to serve, and to lead. That's the shift—seeing "impossible" as a signpost, not a stop sign. And once you see yourself that way, the world starts to open in ways you couldn't have planned, but you're more than ready to meet.

Breaking the Barrier of Self-Doubt

Self-doubt is a silent thief. It convinces you you're not ready, not capable, not enough. For me, the turning point was realizing the real barrier wasn't a lack of opportunity—it was the story I was telling myself about what I could and couldn't do. Once I changed the story, the ceiling moved.

I began with small, deliberate experiments. If a task made me uncomfortable, I did it anyway—*on purpose*—to collect proof that my fear wasn't the final word. Then I invited my employees to do the same. We didn't wait to "feel confident." We acted first and let confidence catch up.

Rewriting the Script, Together

One of the most defining seasons of my career came when I became the general manager of a predominantly Hispanic McDonald's. I was the only English-speaking manager, and communication was a daily hurdle. We could have let that gap divide us. Instead, we built a bridge.

We turned the restaurant into a classroom and a lab. They taught me Spanish while I worked the grill; I taught English while they rotated through service positions. Every station became a vocabulary lesson. Every shift became an exercise in empathy. We didn't just trade words—we traded perspective and pride.

McDonald's launched **English Under the Arches** to help employees learn English, and I had the privilege of watching several team members' graduate. I'll never forget one employee—later promoted to assistant manager—crying happy tears after buying her first home and being able to *read every word* of the closing documents herself. Today, every one of my Under the Arches graduates is a general manager or higher. If that isn't proof that "impossible" can become "I'm possible," I don't know what is.

What That Season Taught Me

- **Self-doubt shrinks when evidence grows.** We didn't "motivate" confidence; we *generated* it by doing hard things in small, repeatable ways.

- **Vulnerability is a leadership skill.** Admitting, "I'm learning Spanish," gave my team permission to admit, "I'm learning English." Shared learning built mutual respect.

- **Psychological safety fuels performance.** When people feel safe to try, fail, and try again, they take smart risks—and grow faster.

- **Skill-building beats stereotyping.** Talent often hides behind language barriers, job titles, or past labels. Investing in skills uncovers it.

The Playbook We Used

- **Micro-commitments:** One new phrase per shift. One new station per week. Small wins, stacked.

- **Buddy system:** Pair an English learner with a Spanish learner; each teaches the other for 15 minutes daily.

- **Job-rotation as training:** Each position = new words + new responsibilities. Language tied to action sticks longer.

- **Celebrate progress publicly:** We

  didn't just celebrate promotions.

Try This (for Your Team or Yourself)

1. **Name the story.** Write the limiting sentence you tell yourself (e.g., "I'm not ready for X").

2. **Shrink the risk.** Design a 10–15- minute experiment you can do this week to test that belief.

3. **Collect proof.** Log what went right. Repeat weekly with slightly bigger challenges.

4. **Share the climb.** Invite a peer or your team to set—and celebrate— micro- goals together.

Self-doubt didn't disappear for me; it learned it no longer runs the show. Every time I witness someone cross a barrier they once believed was fixed—language, confidence, title, background—I'm reminded:

"Impossible" is usually just something we haven't figured out how to do—yet. And once one person crosses, the path is easier for everyone who follows.

Preparation + Faith

Believing *"I'm possible"* isn't about blind optimism. It's about pairing **belief** with **preparation,** so your confidence is earned, not imagined. When I stepped into healthcare operations, I threw myself into learning— compliance standards, medical terminology, HIPAA requirements, insurance processes, and the policies that shape the patient's journey. I didn't wait for someone to hand me the knowledge; I went and got it.

At the call center I led, we built a culture around **readiness** and **belief**. We trained until our team could confidently handle any patient, provider, or insurance call. That preparation gave them faith in their abilities; their faith gave them the courage to perform at a consistently high standard. Patient satisfaction climbed. Employee retention improved.

Quality stabilized. The team believed they could deliver excellence—and then they did.

"Preparation builds the runway; faith gives you the courage to take off." – Heather Williams

Faith without action is wishful thinking. Action without faith is burnout. The magic happens when you have both—**a practiced skillset and a practiced mindset**.

Case Study: The 12-Week Turnaround Context:

When COVID-era backlogs collided with a new rollout, our call center faced spiking volumes, inconsistent answers, and frayed morale. Wait times were up, abandon rates were climbing, and agents felt overwhelmed.

What we did (Preparation):

- **Mapped the journey** (Weeks 1–2): We whiteboard the full call flow— from intake to scheduling to clinical handoff—and identified the five most common failure points.

- **Built a living knowledge base** (Weeks 3–4): One source of truth with plain-language answers, updated daily, searchable in under five seconds.

- **Microlearning sprints** (Weeks 5–6): 10-minute lessons (HIPAA refreshers, insurance triage cues, empathy scripting) embedded at the start of each shift.

- **QA + coaching loops** (Weeks 7–8): Calibrated quality standards; shifted QA from "gotcha" to "growth," with same-day feedback and peer shadowing.

- **Pilot + scale** (Weeks 9–10): A small cross-trained "tiger team" tested new workflows, then trained the floor.

- **Stabilize + celebrate** (Weeks 11–12): We locked in what worked, retired what didn't, and publicized wins— small and large—to reinforce momentum.

What changed (Faith):

- Agents trusted the process because it **worked in practice**, not just on paper.

- Supervisors coached to **strengths**, not just to mistakes.

- Daily huddles reframed the day:

  "Here's what we know, here's what might change, here's how we'll handle it."

Outcomes:

- Service levels stabilized and hit targets consistently for the first time that year.

- Abandon rates dropped as callers got faster, clearer answers.

- Patient satisfaction improved as empathy scripting and accurate information became the norm.

- Retention rose as stress fell, and competence grew.

A moment that mattered:

An essential worker called our center upset after receiving a lab bill for a COVID-19 test. Their employer required frequent testing—especially when symptoms appeared—and they believed, based on their plan communications at the time, that diagnostic COVID testing should have been covered with no out-of-pocket cost. They couldn't afford the bill, and the call opened at a boil.

Our agent led with de-escalation: acknowledged the frustration, apologized for the confusion, and promised to own the issue end-to-end. Then preparation took over. The agent pulled the patient's benefits for the exact date of service and reviewed the payer's guidance in effect then. Within minutes, they spotted the problem.

Working with billing in real time, the agent requested a corrected claim—adding the appropriate diagnosis linkage and billing modifier, updating the place-of-service detail, and attaching a brief payer note for reprocessing. Before ending the call, the agent set a follow-up, placed the account in hold status to prevent collections, and explained the step-by-step timeline so the patient felt informed rather than stranded.

Days later, the payer reprocessed the claim and reduced the patient responsibility to $0 under the plan's COVID testing provisions in effect for that date of service. The patient ended relieved; the agent ended proud. That's **preparation + faith** in action—calm the person, verify the facts, fix the claim, and close the loop.

The Preparation Playbook (Use This)

- **Learn the system:** Take ownership of the rules, tools, and acronyms. Knowing *why* builds confident *how*.
- **Make the right answer easy:** One knowledge base, plain language, updated daily.
- **Train small, train often:** Ten minutes a day beats two hours once a month.
- **Coach for belief:** Catch people doing it right; reinforce the behavior you want repeated.
- **Show the score:** Visible KPIs (service level, FCR, quality) and what specific actions move them.

- **Celebrate traction:** Recognize micro- wins—first call resolved, fastest accurate transfer, clearest documentation.

"Faith says 'I can.' Preparation proves 'I will.' Together, they make 'I did.'"- Heather Williams

Bottom line: Preparation gives you the tools. Faith gives you the lift. When you practice both, "impossible" becomes a starting line— not a stop sign.

Case Study: The Pandemic Response

— Office to Work-From-Home at Scale

When COVID-19 hit, our call center was thrown into uncharted territory almost overnight. Phone lines lit up, safety protocols changed by the hour, and we faced a single, urgent mandate: **move an office-first workforce to remote operations—fast— without compromising, quality, or compliance.**

This wasn't just about moving desks. It was about **re-engineering how we worked**: technology, security, coaching, culture, and measures of success.

Phase 1: Stabilize the Lines

- **Rapid escalation path:** A visible "raise hand" channel for agents to pull in supervisors instantly on anything billing.

  Why it mattered: We needed callers to reach a human, agents to reach a leader, and leaders to reach answers—without lag.

Phase 2: Equip & Secure the Home Office

- **Hardware & connectivity:** Issued, USB headsets with noise cancelation, and softphone licenses. Staggered curbside pickup + direct shipping. Posted "minimum home internet" guidelines and a DIY speed/QoS check.
- **Telephony & QoS:** Moved agents to cloud ACD/softphone; prioritized voice traffic; enabled skills-based routing.
- **Security & compliance (HIPAA):**
  o Enforced MFA + VPN; full- disk encryption; auto-lock screens.
  o "Clean desk" at home: no PHI on paper, no personal devices in earshot, privacy screens if others were present.

- Refreshed policies on call recording, identity verification, and no local downloads/printing.
- **At-home readiness checklist:** Quiet space, stable power/backup plan, headset test, webcam optional.

Why it mattered: Remote work only works when **voice quality, data security, and identity verification** are rock-solid.

Phase 3: Train for a Remote Rhythm

Microlearning sprints: 10-minute daily modules (refreshers, insurance triage cues, empathy scripting for anxious callers).

- **Virtual shadowing & buddy system:** New hires paired with veterans; side- by-side done via screenshare + whisper coaching.
- **Cadence & visibility:**
- **Daily huddles** (15 minutes): priorities, updates, shout-outs.
- **Midday office hours**: live Q&A with a supervisor.
- **End-of-day wrap**: what we saw, what we'll fix by morning.
- **Performance re-grounding:** We adjusted expectations to remote reality—balanced AHT with first-call resolution and accuracy; made **quality + empathy** the north star.

Why it mattered: In remote settings, **short, frequent training** and a predictable rhythm beat long meetings every time.

Phase 4: Optimize & Humanize Knowledge base 2.0: Search in <5 seconds;

playbooks for "most frequent issues".

- **QA as coaching, not "gotcha":**

  Same-day feedback loops; calibrated scoring focused on clarity, compliance, and compassion.

- **Well-being practices:** Quiet hours, no-meeting blocks, camera-optional policy, EAP reminders, and weekly pulse checks to catch burnout early.

- **Belonging online:** Virtual coffee breaks, peer recognition, and "win of the week" stories to keep morale up when distance made people feel alone.

Why it mattered: Sustained performance requires **psychological safety**, not just scripts and dashboards.

What Changed (and Stuck)

- **Service levels** returned to target as remote workflows stabilized.

- **Abandon rates** fell as callback windows and smarter routing absorbed peaks.

- **Patient satisfaction** rose with clearer answers and more consistent empathy.

- **Retention** improved as stress dropped, and competence grew; hiring widened with remote talent.

- **Compliance posture** held firm: no PHI breaches, clean audits, faster remediation cycles.

Lessons We'll Never Unlearn

- **Make the right answer easy.** One knowledge base, plain language, ruthless updating.

- **Coach confidence, not just metrics.** People perform better when they feel safe to try.

- **Short, frequent touchpoints > long meetings.** Cadence creates calm.

- **Security is a behavior.** Tools matter, but so do rituals (clean desk, screen lock, identity checks).

- **Culture is built on purpose.** Tie every script, metric, and policy to what it means for the patient.

We didn't just survive the shift to remote work—we learned to **lead differently**: with clearer processes, stronger compliance, and deeper compassion. The office walls came down, but our standards didn't. In many ways, **we became more connected** than we had been in cubicles—because we designed connection into the work.

Practical Exercise: The Possibility Audit

1. Write down something you currently believe is impossible.
2. List five small steps you could take to make it less impossible.
3. Commit to doing the first one this week.

Closing Thought

The difference between *impossible* and *possible* is almost always perspective and persistence. Perspective asks, *"What else could this mean? What haven't we tried?"* Persistence answers, *"One more step."* You don't have to see the whole road to move forward; you only need enough light for the next stride.

When doubt shows up, shrink the problem until it's movable. Turn a mountain into a series of hills: one call, one email, one conversation, one improved habit. Progress compounds quietly, and what felt unthinkable yesterday becomes ordinary tomorrow.

"The path appears to the person who keeps walking." – Heather Williams

Remember this simple rhythm:

- **Reframe:** Ask a better question—*How can I? Who can help? What's the first inch?*
- **Prepare:** Get the facts, the skills, and the tools you need for the next step.
- **Persist:** Do the small thing now. Then do the next small thing.
- **Reflect:** Capture the win, however tiny, and let it fuel the next move.

You won't always know the timing, but you can own the direction. You won't control every outcome, but you can control your attitude, your effort, and your integrity. Keep your perspective wide, your steps short, and your persistence steady.

Believe the path exists—and keep walking until your feet prove it.

Chapter 3 – Mediocrity

Mediocrity is not failure.

It's a **temporary stage**—a resting point on the path from starting out to becoming extraordinary. It's not where you have to stay, but it's often where you quietly build the **skills, resilience, and clarity** that will carry you higher. Think of mediocrity like a training plateau at the gym: it's the body's way of stabilizing before the next jump in strength.

You haven't stalled—you're consolidating.

Too often, people hear the word *mediocrity* and treat it like a **permanent label**, as if it defines their worth or forecasts their future. But mediocrity simply means you **haven't yet reached your full potential**. It's a **signal, not a sentence**—a dashboard light saying, "It's time to tune, adjust, and grow."

The truth is that every growth curve has flat spots. Champions have average days. Great teams have average quarters. Those seasons don't cancel excellence; they **prepare** it. In mediocrity, you learn the basics so deeply that they become automatic. You build discipline when no one is clapping. You gather honest feedback, strengthen weak links, and practice under low stakes so you can perform under high stakes.

"Mediocrity isn't a verdict—it's a checkpoint. Use it to refuel, retool, and then go again." – Heather Williams

How to turn mediocrity into momentum

- **Name it without shame.** "We're steady, not soaring—yet." Honesty frees energy for change.

- **Run a small-steps audit.** Identify one process, one habit, and one relationship to improve this week.

- **Raise the floor before the ceiling.** Make the worst day better—consistency beats occasional brilliance.

- **Collect proof of progress.** Track tiny wins (response time, quality points, one new skill). Small gains stack.

- **Invite friction.** Seek specific feedback from people who will tell you the truth. Fix one thing at a time.

Leaders, especially, should reframe mediocrity for their teams: normalize the plateau, **highlight progress**, and set **clear next standards**. When people believe average is a place to pass through—not a place to live—they start asking a better question: *What more can we do?* And that question, asked consistently, is how ordinary becomes extraordinary.

Seeing Mediocrity for What It Is

Being average isn't the enemy—it's a snapshot of where you are today. In any healthy operation, the middle of the bell curve provides **stability**. Not everyone will be a top performer, and that's okay. The "average" contributors often carry crucial knowledge, keep processes humming, and absorb routine volume so specialists can focus on high- complexity work. They're the continuity that prevents a good day from becoming a bad one.

Think of a **Gemba walk** (from Lean: "go to the place where work happens"). When you walk the front line and watch the real flow—calls, orders, handoffs—you see what dashboards can't show. You notice how "average" performers:

- Keep queues moving by following the playbook reliably.

- Spot small defects early because they live in the details.

- Model consistency for new hires who need a steady example.

- Maintain culture with everyday behaviors—greeting customers, documenting correctly, escalating on time.

As the saying goes, **"When you're green, you're growing. When you're ripe, you rot."** A team with room to grow is a team with potential. "Average" is often just **unfinished excellence**—skills in progress, confidence not yet built, systems not yet streamlined. Those average moments aren't the end; they're the **starting line** for something better.

In fast food, an "average" shift lead who never misses a temp check or a cleaning cycle keeps the store inspection-ready—quiet excellence that protects brand and safety. In healthcare, an "average" agent who follows verification steps exactly prevents claim denials and protects patients from surprise bills. Neither action trends on a leaderboard, but both **save time, money, and trust**.

Leaders go wrong when they treat mediocrity as a fixed identity instead of a **development stage**. The question isn't "Why aren't you a top performer?" It's "What precise support, clarity, or practice would lift your next metric?" Progress happens when we raise the **floor** (the worst day gets better) before we chase the **ceiling** (occasional brilliance).

What to look for on a Gemba walk

- **Flow blockers:** Where do tasks pause? What info is always missing?
- **Micro-variations:** How do high, mid, and low performers do the same step differently?
- **Signal-to-noise:** What scripts or tools add noise instead of clarity?
- **Friction in handoffs:** Where do errors cluster—before, during, or after the handoff?
- **Bright spots:** Which small behaviors correlate with fewer reworks or faster resolution?

How to lift the middle—practically

- **Make the right way the easy way:** One living knowledge base, plain language, <5-second search.

- **Coach one behavior at a time:** "Next best action" beats general advice.

- **Use peer modeling:** Pair steady "average" doers with new hires—consistency is contagious.

- **Show the score + the lever:** "Here's your QA trend; here's the one change that moves it."

- **Celebrate reliability:** Publicly recognize on-time documentation, clean handoffs, and zero-defect days.

"Average is potential in progress. Treat it like a waypoint, not a destination." – Heather Williams

When you see mediocrity clearly—without shame, with specificity—you unlock momentum. The middle of the team isn't dead weight; it's **latent capacity**. Invest there, and you don't just create a few stars—you **raise the tide** that lifts everyone!

Mediocrity as a Steppingstone

In my own career, I've had seasons where I was steady but not spectacular. I wasn't breaking records or reinventing the wheel. I was showing up, doing the work, and quietly building the foundation for what was to come. At the time, it felt ordinary. Looking back, it was essential.

Those seasons were **invaluable**. They gave me space to develop discipline without the pressure of the spotlight. They allowed room to make mistakes and learn from them without risking collapse. They taught me that consistency is not the enemy of greatness— it's the **precondition** for it. Skill by skill, habit by habit, the "average" phases forged the muscle memory I needed when bigger opportunities arrived.

Think of it like the **S-curve of growth**: there's a slow climb while you learn the basics, a rapid rise when compounding kicks in, and then a plateau where you consolidate before the next climb. That consolidation—the part most people label "mediocre"—is where you hardwire the right behaviors, so they hold under pressure.

"Mediocrity becomes momentum the moment you decide to use it."
– Heather Williams

A quiet season that changed everything

(Fast Food → Healthcare)

There was a stretch at McDonald's when our store was… fine. Not failing, not flying.

Instead of chasing a flashy turnaround, we worked on **raising the floor**:

- We standardized opening/closing checklists, so the worst day got better.

- We measured drive-thru times by hour and adjusted staffing in 15-minute blocks.

- We cross-trained one station per person per week so coverage stayed smooth.

When I later moved into healthcare, those same "ordinary" disciplines translated directly:

- Drive-thru times became **average handle time**; accurate orders became **first-call resolution**.

- Checklists became **HIPAA verification steps** and **scheduling huddles**.

- Cross-training became **multi-skill queues** that protected service levels during spikes.

None of that felt glamorous. All of it built the capability to perform when the stakes rose.

That's what it means to use mediocrity as a steppingstone.

Turn the plateau into a springboard (How- to)

1. **Name the season without shame** "We're steady, not soaring—yet." Honesty frees energy for change.

2. **Raise the floor before the ceiling**

   Make the worst day better: tighte

handoffs, fix one recurring defect, shorten one delay.

3. **Stack one skill at a time**

   Choose a single behavior to master this week (e.g., verification script, documentation clarity). Reps > intensity.

4. **Install feedback loops**

   Quick scorecards, same-day coaching, peer shadowing. Small corrections, often.

5. **Track tiny wins**

   One-point QA gains, one-minute AHT drops, one fewer rework—proof that progress is real.

6. **Crosstrain deliberately**

   Broaden competence so the team is resilient. Redundancy is quiet excellence.

7. **Celebrate reliability**

   Applaud no-error days, clean audits, on-time closes—not just record highs.

A mini case: The "average" month that moved the needle.

In one healthcare team, we dedicated a single month to "boring" improvements:

- Simplified the knowledge base to a one-page quick-answer view.
- Rewrote two confusing scripts using plain language.

- Added a 10-minute daily practice of the top five call scenarios.

By month's end, **first-call resolution** ticked up, **QA** rose, and **stress** went down. No heroic overhaul—just steady, ordinary work compounding into meaningful results.

If you treat mediocrity as a **training ground**, it becomes the bridge to extraordinary performance—**if you're willing to keep growing**. The plateau isn't a prison; it's a platform. Stand on it, stack skills, and take the next step.

Asking the Right Question

When you find yourself in a season of mediocrity, the most powerful question you can ask is: **"What more can I do?"**

Ask it with curiosity, not judgment—let it turn a plateau into a plan. Identify one small lever you can pull this week (a clearer script, a cleaner handoff, a five-minute practice) and commit to it. Measure a simple result, however tiny, to prove progress to yourself.

Repeat the cycle, and "average for now" becomes "advancing on purpose." Asked with curiosity—not criticism—this question turns a plateau into a plan. It shifts your brain from judgment to problem-solving, from *why I'm stuck* to *how I move*. The danger isn't being average for a moment—it's staying there because you never push for more.

"The difference between stagnation and momentum is one honest question asked daily." – Heather Williams

Turn "more" into something measurable!

Break "more" into specific levers you can actually pull:

- **Scope:** What small slice can I own end-to-end this week?
- **Leverage:** What task, if improved by 10%, would improve everything else?
- **Learning:** What skill—script, system, policy—would remove the most friction if I mastered it?
- **Relationships:** Who, if I partnered with them, would help us move faster or smarter?
- **Systems:** What checklist, template, or shortcut would prevent repeat mistakes?
- **Constraints:** What rule is real, and

  what's just a habit we can redesign?
- **Impact:** What action would help the patient/customer the most, the soonest? Pick one lever. Define one action. Do it within seven days.

Two quick examples

Fast food → Drive-thru delay

- *Question:* "What more can we do in the next hour?"
- *Action:* Move the best multitasker to assembly during peak; pre-stage condiments; adjust staffing in 15- minute blocks.
- *Result:* Cut average window time by 12–20 seconds—no policy change required.

Healthcare → First-call resolution

- *Question:* "What more can we do before the next shift?"
- *Action:* Create a one-page "Top 5 Scenarios" quick-answer view in the knowledge base; practice 10 minutes in huddle.
- *Result:* Faster, clearer answers; fewer transfers; calmer patients.

The 5-step "MORE" routine (10 minutes, daily)

1. **Mark** one friction point (where you feel slow, stuck, or unsure).
2. **Observe** one cause (missing info, unclear script, handoff gap).
3. **Redesign** one tiny step (a phrase, a checklist, a template).

4. **Execute** today (not next week).

5. **Review** tomorrow (did it help? Keep, tweak, or toss).

Small improvements compound. You don't need a new job to get new momentum—you need a new next step.

Avoid these traps!

- **Self-blame loops:** Replace "Why can't I...?" with "How could I...?"
- **Perfectionism:** Ship the 80% fix today; iterate to 95% later.
- **Comparison:** Benchmark behaviors,

  not worth. Learn, don't label.
- **Trying five things at once:** Change one behavior; measure one result.

Make it a weekly habit (15 minutes, Fridays)

- **Name the plateau:** Where were we steady, not soaring?
- **Pick one lever:** Scope, leverage, learning, relationships, systems, constraints, or impact.
- **Set one metric:** Seconds saved, errors reduced, follow-ups prevented.
- **Schedule one rep:** Put it on the calendar before you log off.

"Ask 'What more can I do?' until the answer becomes 'More than I believed yesterday.'" - Heather Williams

When you get specific about "more," mediocrity becomes motion. The question creates focus. The first step creates evidence. And evidence—stacked day after day— creates the momentum that carries you from average to extraordinary.

The McDonald's Lesson

Early in my management career at McDonald's, our store's performance was… fine. We hit targets, kept customers satisfied, and avoided major problems—but we weren't excelling. "Fine" is comfortable. It's also where momentum goes to sleep.

One day, I gathered the team for a five-minute huddle and asked a single question:

"What's one thing we can do better this week?"

That tiny shift—from maintaining to improving—sparked a roll of changes. Not a grand makeover, just small, specific moves we could test fast and keep if they worked.

What changed first?

- **Drive-thru flow:** We pre-staged common condiments, moved our fastest multitasker to assembly during peak, and added a "runner" at the window to reduce handoffs. Seconds started melting off our service time.

- **Prep simplification:** We color-coded bins, relabeled shelves in plain language, and set par levels by time of day. Less hunting, more doing.

- **Clean-as-you-go:** We created a "first 5 / last 5" checklist—first five minutes of a shift and last five minutes dedicated to zone resets. Dining room standards improved without extra labor.

- **Cross-training:** Each person learned one new station per week. Coverage got easier, breaks got smoother, and team empathy grew because everyone knew each other's pain points.

How we kept it moving

- **Gemba moments:** Once a day, we walked the line for five minutes, watching the real flow: where hands reached twice, where a step was missing, where someone waited. We fixed *that* next.

- **One lever at a time:** Each week had a theme—assembly, cleanliness, order accuracy, headset etiquette—so focus stayed sharp.

- **Visible scoreboards:** A whiteboard with three simple metrics (service time, accuracy, customer comments) made progress feel real. We circled wins in green and circled opportunities in blue with a single next action.

- **Recognition in public, coaching in private:** "Win of the day" shout-outs in huddles-built pride. Quiet 1:1 coaching built skill.

Within months, customer satisfaction scores climbed, sales followed, and—more importantly—the team began to take pride in beating their *own* best results. The store didn't transform because we demanded perfection. It transformed because we believed we could do **one thing better each week**, and then we proved it.

"Excellence isn't a leap; it's a stack of small, kept promises." - Heather Williams

Why this mattered (then and later)

- We learned to **raise the floor**—to make the worst day better—before chasing record highs.
- We learned that **clarity beats intensity**: one goal, one lever, one scoreboard.
- We learned that **ownership is contagious**: when people see their idea work on Tuesday, they bring another on Friday.

Those lessons followed me into healthcare. Drive-thru seconds became average handle time, order accuracy became first-call resolution, checklists became HIPAA-safe verification flows. Different industry, same engine: ask a better question, pick one lever, move it together, measure aloud, repeat.

It wasn't about chasing perfection overnight— it was about believing we could do more, then building a rhythm that made "more" inevitable.

Mediocrity is Not the End

In healthcare operations, I've seen "average" teams become top-tier units. The shift never came from demanding instant perfection. It came from **consistent, meaningful improvement**—one behavior, one process, one decision at a time.

When you treat mediocrity as a **checkpoint** instead of a dead end, you stop defending the current standard and start asking, *What's the next right lever to pull?* That question changes everything. It moves people from fear to ownership, from stagnation to motion.

"Raise the floor first; the ceiling will follow." - Heather Williams

What the transformation actually looks like

- **Clarity:** Define the few outcomes that matter (e.g., first-call resolution, accuracy, patient sentiment).

- **Focus:** Pick **one** behavior to improve this week (verification script, escalation criteria, note quality).

- **Feedback:** Short, frequent coaching beats long, rare meetings.

- **Proof:** Make progress visible—tiny wins on a whiteboard or dashboard build belief.

- **Repeat:** Keep the cycle tight: learn → apply → measure → refine.

Mini-Case: From Middle of the Pack to Model Team (8 Weeks)

Starting point: Mid-performing call center pod. KPIs were "okay": FCR ~78%, QA 94%. **Week 1–2 – One script, one standard:** We rewrote a script in plain language and practiced 10 minutes at every huddle.

Week 3–4 – Handoff hygiene: Standardized warm transfers and note templates to eliminate rework.

Week 5–6 – Knowledge base quick- answers: Built a one-page view for the top five call scenarios; search in <5 seconds.

Week 7–8 – QA as coaching: Same-day

feedback; celebrate "clean calls" publicly.

Results:

- FCR from 78% → **88%**

- QA from 94% → **97%**
- Patient sentiment shifted from neutral to **consistently positive.**
- Stress dropped; retention stabilized.

No heroics—just a steady rise driven by clear focus and small, durable changes.

Practical Exercise: The Mediocrity Mindset Shift (Expanded)

Use this as a one-week sprint you can repeat monthly.

Step 1 — Identify one "average" area Pick a spot where you feel steady but not strong (e.g., follow-ups, documentation clarity, response time, a relationship you've let drift).

Step 2 — Define the lever and the metric.

- *Lever:* What single behavior would improve this area?
- *Metric:* What number will tell you it's working? (seconds saved, errors reduced, fewer transfers, quicker handoffs)

Step 3 — Design a micro-action (daily, <15 minutes)

Examples:

- Rewrite one confusing sentence in a script.

- Build a 3-line checklist for a frequent task.

- Do a 10-minute roleplay on the most common scenario.

- Pair with a peer for one "listen-in" and

  one tip.

  Step 4 — Execute for 5 business days Keep it small, consistent, and visible. Track results at the end of each day.

  Step 5 — Review & lock the gain (15 minutes, Day 6)

- What improved? What felt easier?

- Keep what worked; tweak or drop

  what didn't.

- Set the *next* micro-action for the following week.

  Optional team version

- Share one micro-win in huddle.

- Post a tiny metric (e.g., "3 fewer reworks today").

- Recognize reliability, not just speed.

  Watchouts

- Don't change five things at once—**one lever** per week.

- Don't wait for perfect—shift the 80% fix and iterate.

- Don't compare worth—compare **behaviors** and learn.

"Momentum is mediocrity practiced with intention." – Heather Williams

Treat "average" as **unfinished excellence**. When you raise the floor with small, repeatable wins, the ceiling moves on its own. That's how teams—and people—cross the bridge from mediocrity to extraordinary.

Closing Thought

Failing to meet the mark doesn't mean you've failed—it means you've reached a moment of choice. You can label it a dead end, or you can treat it as data: feedback about what to try next, what skill to sharpen, what support to seek. Every miss gives you another chance to try, to try harder, and—most importantly—to believe again in what's possible.

Mediocrity can be the **bridge** between where you are and the extraordinary future waiting for you. On that bridge, you build stamina, refine fundamentals, and learn to show up when no one is clapping. That quiet consistency becomes your unfair advantage when the next opportunity appears.

"A setback is not a stop sign—it's a signpost pointing to the next step." - Heather Williams

If you're standing on that bridge today, don't rush past it. Use it:

- **Name the lesson.** What did this attempt teach you?
- **Pick one lever.** What single behavior will you improve this week?
- **Stack small wins.** Let consistency, not perfection, move the needle.

You don't have to leap to greatness—you have to **walk** toward it, one deliberate step at a time. Keep your belief intact, your actions steady, and your eyes on the horizon. The mark you missed today can become the momentum you ride tomorrow.

CHAPTER 4 –

Extraordinary in the Ordinary

When we hear the word *extraordinary*, most of us picture something grand—standing ovations, groundbreaking inventions, or record-breaking achievements. But in my experience, the most extraordinary moments often hide inside the everyday, quietly shaping lives without fanfare.

The truth is that greatness rarely bursts onto the scene with fireworks. More often, it's built through small, consistent actions—decisions and habits so ordinary at the time that you barely notice their power... until you look back and realize they changed everything.

At McDonald's, I consistently delivered the basics—and the basics delivered me. Over the years I received awards like **"Making a Positive Difference," "Best Retention," "Most Profitable,"** and **"Outstanding Restaurant Manager."** Those weren't the result of magic days; they were the product of **ordinary operations done well every day**— food safety checks on time, prep lines ready, labor schedules aligned to volume, clean dining rooms, and respectful coaching. The impact was extraordinary because it was reliable. Employees felt supported. Customers got what they needed, when they needed it, without drama.

You could walk into one of my restaurants on any given day, see the same faces, and get the **same results**—consistency you could count on. I often think of the **Publix** experience: you can walk into any Publix grocery store, and the service *feels* the same—steady, friendly, dependable. That kind of brand trust isn't built by stunts; it's built by standards. I pursued the same philosophy at McDonald's and carried it into healthcare.

When I transitioned to the call center, I applied the same playbook: **reliable processes, clear standards, and everyday excellence.** An "ordinary" team became an extraordinary one—not overnight, but predictably—because we made the right way the easy way and held to it. We launched a one-page knowledge base for top scenarios, standardized warm transfers and note hygiene, and practiced ten-minute huddles each day.

Within weeks, first-call resolution and QA climbed while escalations dropped, and patients reported clearer answers and calmer calls. Consistency did the heavy lifting—we just kept showing up the right way.

Ordinary, Systematized

Extraordinary outcomes emerge when you systematize ordinary excellence:

- **Standards over slogans:** Replace "work hard" with three visible standards (e.g., temp logs by the hour, drive-thru staging checklist, clean-as- you-go zones).

- **Right people, right seats:** Schedule to demand curves; staff strengths to peak windows.

- **One source of truth:** Keep a single, always-updated guide (recipes/scripts/policies) in plain language.

- **Daily rhythm:** First 5 / Last 5 minutes for resets; 10-minute huddles for priorities and praise.

- **Coach to behavior, not personality:** "One change today" beats general advice.

- **Celebrate reliability:** Shine a light on on-time checks, clean audits, zero- defect days—not only record highs.

"Excellence is ordinary work done on purpose—again tomorrow."
– Heather Williams

From Burgers to Bedside (via Headsets)

What translated from McDonald's to

healthcare call centers:

- **Throughput → Access:** Drive-thru time became **Average Handle Time**; order accuracy became **First-Call Resolution**.

- **Food safety → Compliance:** Temperature logs became **HIPAA verification steps** and secure documentation.

- **Prep lines → Knowledge lines:** Prepped stations became a **one-page knowledge base** for top call scenarios.

- **Shift huddles → Clinical cadence:** 10-minute huddles aligned staffing, priorities, and empathy scripts.

- **Zone cleaning → Error-proofing:** Clean-as-you-go became **clean handoffs**—no missing notes, no mystery tickets.

Results you can feel: Service stabilized, abandon rates dropped, QA and patient sentiment rose, and the team's confidence— and retention—climbed. Nothing flashy. Just ordinary excellence compounding into extraordinary reliability for patients.

A Mini-Case: Making Ordinary Exceptional

Starting point: A mid-performing pod with uneven answers and rising stress.

Three ordinary moves:

1. **One-page quick answers** for the top five call types (findable in <5 seconds).

2. **Warm transfer standard** with a shared note template (no cold handoffs).

3. **10-minute practice** at each huddle (scripts + empathy for anxious callers).

Eight weeks later: First-Call Resolution up, QA in the 90s, sentiment shifted positive. The "wow" wasn't a single hero moment—it was **consistent accuracy and kindness call after call**.

How to See the Extraordinary (and Make More of It)

- **Zoom out:** Ask, *if we repeated this small action for 90 days, what would move?*
- **Name the gain:** What patient, teammate, or metric improves when we do the basics perfectly?
- **Tighten the loop:** Learn → Apply → Measure → Refine. Weekly.
- **Protect the floor:** Make the worst day better before you chase records.
- **Honor the quiet wins:** Reliability is a result. Treat it like one.

The Hidden Power of Small Acts

During my years in fast food, the "big wins" were obvious—breaking sales records, acing inspections, or hitting corporate benchmarks. But the true victories were often quieter—so small, they could be missed if you weren't looking:

- **A shift that flowed** because teammates watched each other's backs and stepped in before a bottleneck formed.

- **A customer who left smiling** because they were treated like a person, not a transaction—eye contact, a name, a sincere "thank you."

- **An employee trying a new station** and succeeding because someone coached them for five minutes beforehand.

Those moments didn't make headlines, but they created an environment where excellence became the norm. I learned that **ordinary actions, done with care and consistency, are the real building blocks of extraordinary results.** Excellence isn't a single leap; it's a hundred small choices, repeated.

Micro-Behaviors That Move Mountains

In practice, small acts look like this:

- **Pre-stage what's needed next.**
  Napkins, sauces, hot cups, or prep pans set early to prevent later scrambles— and shave seconds when seconds matter.

- **Call the play out loud.** "I've got the window; you take drinks." One clear line sets the entire pace.

- **First 5 / Last 5.** Spend the first five minutes resetting your zone; spend the last five leaving it ready for the next person.

- **One phrase of respect.** "Thanks for your patience; here's what I can do right now." Dignity diffuses tension.

- **Coach in the moment.** A 60-second tip between orders sticks better than a 60-minute lecture later.

"Small acts are standards in disguise. Repeat them long enough and they become culture." – Heather Williams

A Small Act, Big Outcome (Fast Food)

One Friday rush, our window times spiked. Nothing "big" was broken—just a string of tiny frictions. We made three micro-moves: assigned a runner for drinks only, pre-staged sauces, and had the assembler call "next two items" aloud. Window time dropped by twenty seconds in the next half hour, and stress fell with it. The fix wasn't heroic; it was **micro and repeatable**.

Translating Small Acts to Healthcare

When I moved into healthcare call centers, those same micro-acts became:

- **Warm transfers** instead of cold handoffs: introduce the patient, summarize the issue in one sentence, and confirm the next step.
- **Single source of truth**: a one-page quick-answer view for the top call types (findable in under five seconds).
- **Identity + empathy first**: verify PHI, then acknowledge fear or frustration before problem-solving.
- **Note hygiene**: clear, consistent documentation that saves the next person five minutes—and saves the patient from repeating their story.
- **Ten-minute huddles**: one skill, one update, one shout-out—daily.

The results felt extraordinary to patients (fewer repeats, clearer answers, calmer calls) but were built from ordinary acts executed predictably.

Why Small Acts Work (The Physics of Operations)

- **They hit leading indicators.** Small acts improve the steps that *create* outcomes (flow, handoffs, clarity), which then lift the metrics everyone cares about.

- **They're teachable.** People can adopt a small behavior today—and keep it tomorrow.

- **They compound.** Five seconds saved per call adds up across a day, a week, a team.

- **They lower stress.** Predictable moves reduce surprises, which calms both staff and customers/patients.

The Small-Act Playbook (Use This)

1. **Pick one friction point.** (Where do we always slow down?)
2. **Design one micro-fix.** (A phrase, a checklist line, a pre-stage moves.)
3. **Practice for five minutes.** (In huddle or side-by-side.)
4. **Run it for a week.** (Same fix, every shift.)
5. **Measure one number.** (Seconds saved, reworks avoided, transfers reduced.)
6. **Keep, tweak, or toss.** (If it works, turn it into a standard.)

Bottom line: Small acts don't look extraordinary while you're doing them. But when you look back—at calmer shifts, happier customers, fewer errors, and a team that trusts each other—you see their power. Do the ordinary with intention, and the results will look like magic to everyone else.

Healthcare: Where the Ordinary Saves Lives

(Patient Customer Service — Revenue Cycle Management)

When I transitioned into healthcare operations, the lesson became undeniable: what looks *ordinary* on our side of the phone often feels **life-altering** on the patient's side. In a billing-focused call center, the work isn't just about balances and statements—it is about **access**. A clear explanation can mean the difference between a patient delaying care out of fear and a patient scheduling the appointment they need.

In revenue cycle management, every call contains a chain of small, "ordinary" actions: verifying identity, confirming benefits, explaining an EOB, fixing a coordination-of- benefits issue, or setting up a payment plan. None of those steps feel heroic—but together, they **remove barriers to care**. They lower anxiety, prevent collections harm, and keep patients engaged in their health journey.

"In billing, we don't just resolve balances— we restore people's ability to say 'yes' to care." – Heather Williams

Why the "Ordinary" Matters in RCM

- **Tone → Trust:** The first 30 seconds either calm a patient or hardens their fear. A calm voice and a clear promise— *"I'll own this with you"*— can turn conflict into partnership.

- **Clarity → Compliance with Care:** Patients who understand what they owe (and why) are more likely to keep follow-ups, refill medications, and return for preventive visits.

- **Speed → Continuity:** Quick follow- ups on authorizations, claim reprocessing, or financial assistance can prevent gaps in treatment.

- **Accuracy → Access:** Clean demographics, correct plan/ID, right modifiers, and place-of-service details—these "mundane" details stop denials and surprise bills before they start.

What It Looked Like Day to Day

- **EOB Translation:** We turned payer language into plain English: *"This isn't a bill; it is the plan's summary.*

Here is what they paid, what they did not, and why."

- **Financial Navigation:** For true out-of- pocket costs, we offered **payment plan** options—and we followed through until the account was safe from collections.

Micro-Behaviors That Move Outcomes

- **Identity + Empathy First:** Verify PHI, then acknowledge the concern before numbers.

- **One-Page "Quick Answer" View:** Top 5 billing scenarios (EOB, deductible vs. copay, PA/denial, COB, self-pay options) findable in under 5 seconds.

- **Standard Phrases:** "Here's what I can do right now." "Let me own this for you." "I'll call you by [date] with an update."

- **Note Hygiene:** Clear, consistent account notes save the next rep five minutes and save the patient five explanations.

- **Same-Day Follow-Ups:** A quick check-back after a fixed claim or new plan info builds confidence and prevents callbacks.

Mini-Case: A Balance That Blocked Care

A patient postponed lab work because of a prior surprise bill. They called angry and scared. The agent listened, apologized for the confusion, and reviewed benefits for the original date of service. In one call, the agent coordinated a **corrected claim**, put the account on **hold** to prevent collections, and **scheduled a check-in**. The payer reprocessed to **$0 patient responsibility** under the correct benefit. The patient scheduled the lab work the same week.

No miracle—just ordinary steps done right: empathy, verification, claim fix, loop closed.

Metrics That Reflect Care (And How We Move Them)

- **First-Call Resolution (FCR):** Clear answers + empowered adjustments = fewer callbacks.

- **Average Handle Time (AHT):** Improves naturally when the **knowledge base** is fast and notes are clean.

- **Right-Party Contacts:** Correct demographics + identity verification reduces misroutes and compliance risk.

- **Denial Rate / Rework:** Front-end accuracy + clean coding = fewer patient bills and better payer yield.

- **Patient Satisfaction:** Measured via brief surveys driven by tone, clarity, and follow through.

The RCM Playbook (You Can Use This)

1. **Make the right answer easy:** One living knowledge base, plain language, daily updates.

2. **Script the first minute:** Verification + empathy + ownership = de-escalation.

3. **Standardize handoffs:** Warm transfers + shared note templates = no patient repeats.

4. **Fix one leak per week:** Pick a common denial, solve the root cause, measure the drop.

5. **Close the loop:** Promise a follow-up— and keep it. Trust is built on callbacks kept.

"Patients don't remember our systems. They remember if we stayed with them till the answer arrived." – Heather Williams

Bottom line: In patient billing and revenue cycle, the "ordinary" work—accurate benefits, clear explanations, clean claims, and compassionate options—**saves care**. It keeps patients from walking away, keeps families out of crisis, and keeps the mission intact. Do these small things well and consistently, and you'll watch ordinary actions produce extraordinary access to health.

Finding Meaning in the Everyday

Extraordinary doesn't always mean doing *more*. Often, it means doing the **basics** so well—and so consistently—that they set a new standard. The magic isn't in rare heroics; it's in reliable habits that customers, patients, and teammates can trust.

One of the most rewarding parts of my leadership journey has been watching people grow simply because someone **believed** in them. That belief—delivered in small, everyday ways through guidance, encouragement, and trust—sparked transformations that no formal program could have forced.

I've seen a quiet cashier turn into a shift trainer because a supervisor spent five minutes a day practicing greetings and flow with them. I've watched a nervous revenue cycle agent go from avoiding Explanation of Benefits (EOB) calls to mentoring others—because we gave her a one-page quick guide, role-played for ten minutes in huddle, and celebrated her first "clean call." None of that made a headline. All of it changed careers.

Belief becomes culture when it's **ritualized**:

- A two-sentence **daily check-in** ("What's one thing I can help unblock today?").

- A **5:1** encouragement-to-coaching ratio (notice five things done right for every one thing to improve).

- A **"why it matters"** story in huddle that connects today's task to a real customer or patient outcome.

- A **first-5 / last-5** habit reset your space for the next person—leave it better than you found it.

"Excellence lives in the unglamorous. Do small things right until they can't be ignored." – Heather Williams

How to See the Extraordinary

Shift Your Perspective

Ask, *If I zoomed out, how would this small action matter in the big picture?*

- Fast food: Pre-staging sauces saves seconds, which lowers wait times, which improves sentiment, which lifts sales.

- Healthcare billing: A clear EOB explanation prevents a second call, which reduces anxiety, which keeps the patient engaged in care.

Celebrate Daily Wins

Don't wait for monumental moments to acknowledge progress.

- Call out "clean handoffs," error-free notes, and on-time closes.
- Post a simple scoreboard: *one* metric moved today and *one* behavior that moved it.

Be Intentional

Treat routine tasks as opportunities to leave things better than you found them.

- Rewrite a confusing sentence in a script.
- Add a single line to a checklist that prevents a common miss.
- Teach one tip to the person next to you before the shift ends.

Practical Ways to Build Meaning (Right Now)

- **The 60-Second Why:** Before a task you do every day, state aloud how it helps a customer/patient or a teammate. Meaning grows where purpose is named.
- **Micro-Mentoring:** Pair for 10 minutes after lunch—each person shares one trick that saved them time this week.

- **Gratitude with Specifics:** "Thank you" + *what, where, and why* ("Your summary note saved the next rep five minutes and the patient from retelling their story").

- **Keep / Tweak / Toss (Weekly):** Pick one tiny process. Decide what to keep, what to tweak, what to toss. Lock the change for a week and measure one number.

"If you can't find the extraordinary, zoom in. It's hiding inside the ordinary you repeat." – Heather Williams

Bottom line: Meaning is manufactured in minutes, not milestones. When you connect daily actions to outcomes—and recognize reliability as real achievement—you turn everyday into a platform for excellence. Over time, those ordinary choices compound into results that look extraordinary to everyone else.

Extraordinary is a Choice

The extraordinary isn't reserved for a select few. It's available to anyone who chooses to value the details and approach each day with intention. You don't need a new title, a bigger budget, or perfect conditions—you need a decision: I will turn ordinary moments into meaningful ones.

Every day offers dozens of small choices: the tone you use, the preparation you do (or skip), the way you close a loop, the care you take with documentation, the patience you bring to a tense conversation. **Those micro-choices stack.** Over time they become trust, consistency, and results that look like "excellence" from the outside.

"Extraordinary is just ordinary done on purpose—and repeated." – Heather Williams

What it looks like in practice

- **Fast food:** Pre-staging condiments, calling the play aloud ("I've got window; you take drinks"), resetting your station in the first and last five minutes of the shift.

- **Healthcare (RCM call center):** Warm transfers instead of cold handoffs, a one-sentence issue summary in the account note, verifying benefits before explaining an EOB, setting, and keeping a follow-up date.

These aren't flashy moves. But they reduce friction, lower stress, and raise confidence— one interaction at a time.

The Extraordinary Audit

Use this once a week. Ten minutes, tops.

Step 1 — List three ordinary tasks you do every week.

Examples:

- Fast food: opening checklist, drive- thru assembly during peak, shift huddle.
- Healthcare RCM: benefits verification, EOB explanation calls.

Step 2 — For each task, brainstorm one way to elevate it.

Prompts:

- What could I **prepare** in advance, so it flows?
- What could I **say** that would add clarity or calm?
- What could I **standardize** so the right way is the easy way?
- What could I **remove** that adds noise without value?

Step 3 — Turn each idea into a tiny, testable change (run for 5 days).

Examples:

- **Fast food:** Add a 10-second "next two items" call at assembly; pre-stage top three sauces during peak; "first-5 /

  last-5" zone reset.
- **Healthcare RCM:** Create a one-line EOB explanation script; add a warm- transfer pledge ("I'll stay on the line to introduce you").

Step 4 — Measure one number per task.

- Seconds saved, reworks avoided, transfers reduced, callbacks prevented, QA points gained, sentiment shift.

Step 5 — Keep / Tweak / Toss.

If it works, make it a standard. If it helps a little, refine it. If it flops, drop it and test the next idea.

Optional 30-Day Sprint

- Week 1: Elevate **preparation** (checklists, pre-staging, quick-answer sheets).
- Week 2: Elevate **communication**

  (scripts, tone, warm handoffs).
- Week 3: Elevate **handoffs** (notes, summaries, follow-up dates).
- Week 4: Elevate **consistency** (daily

  rhythm, huddles, "first-5 / last-5").

Everyday Examples (So It's Real)

- **Fast food:**

o *Ordinary:* Hand the bag and say "thanks."

Extraordinary: Confirm the order by name, hand napkins proactively, and say, "We appreciate you—drive safe." Small seconds; big sentiment.

- **Healthcare RCM:**

o *Ordinary:* "This is your balance."

o *Extraordinary:* "Here's what the plan paid, here's what they didn't, and here's why. I can place the account on hold while we correct this, and I'll call you on Thursday with an update." Anxiety down, trust up, resolution faster.

Closing Thought

Extraordinary rarely arrives in a single leap. It's grown—quietly—from the accumulation of everyday excellence: a hundred small acts, chosen on purpose, repeated until they become who you are. When you train your eyes to see value in the ordinary and raise it by one inch each day, something shifts. You stop chasing "big moments" and start manufacturing momentum. Inch by inch becomes yard by yard; routine becomes reliability; reliability becomes trust; trust becomes impact.

"Excellence is built in inches. Keep the inches, and the miles take care of themselves." - Heather Williams

If you want a practical way to live this:

- **Name one ordinary act** you'll elevate today.

- **Decide one tiny improvement** (a phrase, a checklist line, a prep step).

- **Repeat it for five days** and watch the ripple: calmer calls, cleaner handoffs, clearer outcomes.

You don't need a new title, a perfect plan, or permission. You need one deliberate inch— today—then another tomorrow. Do that long enough and you'll look back and realize the truth that was waiting in you all along: **you were extraordinary—inch by inch—before anyone else could see it.**

Leadership and the Shift from Hard Skills to Soft Skills

True leadership in healthcare isn't about knowing everything—it's about knowing how to bring out the best in the people who do. The most effective leaders don't lead from a pedestal; they lead from within the team, shaping vision, building trust, and influencing the right people to deliver an exceptional patient experience.

In healthcare, the patient's experience is a living, breathing cycle. It begins long before a patient arrives and continues long after they leave: appointment access, pre-visit communications, intake accuracy, clinical handoffs, billing clarity, and compassionate follow-up. To influence excellence in this cycle, you must understand **the moving parts**—and **the people** who move them.

From Hard Skills to Soft Skills (and Why Both Matter)

When I entered healthcare operations, my first wins were "hard skills":

- **Process mapping** the intake → scheduling → authorization → billing flow.

- **KPI literacy** (service level, AHT, FCR, denial rate, clean claim rate)
- **Compliance fluency** (HIPAA, identity verification, documentation standards)
- **Capacity planning** (forecasting volume, staffing to demand curves)

Hard skills stabilize the system. But to **elevate** the system, you need soft skills that shape behavior and culture:

- **Psychological safety:** People speak up about risks and defects.
- **Coaching over correcting:** Build capability, not fear.
- **Strength's alignment:** Put people where they do their best thinking and caring.
- **Empathy and clarity:** Reduce anxiety—for patients and staff—with tone and transparent next steps.
- **Trust and recognition:** What you notice grows; what you celebrate repeats.

"Hard skills make the work possible; soft skills make the work powerful." – Heather Williams

The Leadership Shift (Five Quiet Pivots)

1. **From expert to orchestrator** – Stop being the answer; start building the system that finds answers.

2. **From telling to coaching** – Ask better questions; unlock people's judgment.

3. **From compliance to commitment** – Connect tasks to purpose (patient outcomes, not just metrics).

4. **From audits to attention** – Replace occasional "gotcha" reviews with frequent, supportive check-ins.

5. **From job description to strengths** – Shape roles around what people do best most of the time.

A Marcus Buckingham– Style Case: Strengths Make Systems Stronger

(Principles inspired by Marcus Buckingham's strengths-based work—e.g., *Go Put Your Strengths to Work; Nine Lies About Work; Love + Work*—emphasizing frequent attention, individualized strengths, and teams built around what people do best.)

Setting: Billing/RCM call center struggling with inconsistency—okay service levels, uneven FCR.

Hypothesis: If we redesign the *human* system around individual strengths and weekly attention, hard metrics will improve.

What we changed

- **Weekly strengths check-ins:** Each agent met with a lead to answer three prompts:

1. *What energized you last week?* (lean into it)

2. *What drained you?* (buffer or redesign)

3. *What's your priority this week—and how can I help?*

- **Strengths-based task alignment:**

o Fast pattern-recognizers → benefits/eligibility verification & denial triage

o Warm communicators → EOB explanations, financial- assistance conversations, escalations

o Detail anchors → note hygiene, knowledge-base updates, QA calibration.

- **One-page quick answers:** Built by the "detail anchors," in plain language, findable in <5 seconds for top billing scenarios.

- **QA as coaching:** Same-day feedback focused on *what worked* and *one next behavior.*

- **Recognition loops:** Daily huddle "bright spots" tied to strengths ("your plain-English EOB saved a callback").

  Outcomes:

- **First-Call Resolution**: +8 percentage points

- **QA accuracy**: to 97%+ with fewer reworks
- **Patient sentiment**: shifted positive (calmer calls, clearer next steps)
- **Retention**: improved as agents spent more time in "strength zones"

Why it worked (Buckingham principles in action):

- People grow most where they're already strong; redesign roles to amplify that.
- **Frequent attention** from a team lead beats rare formal feedback.
- Real teams share a purpose and rely on one another's strengths; build the workflow to reflect that reality.

Leadership takeaway: Systems get better when people do more of their best work, more of the time.

Putting It into Practice (Your Playbook)

- **Map the work, then the strengths.** For each step in your patient experience cycle, list the human strengths that make that step sing (e.g., empathy for financial-assistance calls; pattern recognition for denial fixes).

- **Install weekly check-ins.** 15 minutes. Three questions. Every person. Every week.

- **Design strength-aligned lanes.** Keep flexibility, but bias assignments toward energy and excellence.

- **Coach one behavior at a time.** "Next best action" beats vague advice.

- **Celebrate reliability.** Recognize clean handoffs, zero-defect notes, kept follow-ups—not just speed records.

"Build the system around what your people do best, and the system will start doing its best." – Heather Williams

Why This Matters for Patients

Soft skills aren't soft for the patient. A warm tone, a confident explanation, and a kept promise reduce fear—and fear is the enemy of care. When teams work in their strengths, the **ordinary moments** (verification, an EOB explanation, a corrected claim) feel **extraordinary** to the person on the other end of the line. That's leadership and influence at their most practical: **hard skills stabilized, soft skills humanized, outcomes improved.**

Influence Through Relationships (Servant Leadership in Practice)

At the heart of leadership is influence—and at the heart of influence is **relationship- building**. Titles may grant authority, but **relationships earn loyalty**. In my career, I've watched teams move from average to extraordinary not because I demanded more, but because I **invested more**—time, attention, trust, and advocacy.

This is the core of **servant leadership**: the leader's first job is to **serve** the people who serve the mission. You don't stand above the work; you stand **behind** your people, removing friction, securing resources, clarifying the "why," and celebrating progress so they can do their best work for patients.

"If I serve my people well, they'll serve our patients exceptionally."
– Heather Williams

What Servant Leadership Looks Like (Day to Day)

- **Listening before directing:** "Tell me what's in your way," precedes "Here's the plan."
- **Empathy + standards:** High care and high bar—support paired with clear expectations.
- **Persuasion over position:** Win hearts to win habits; explain the "why," invite input, and co-design solutions.
- **Growth as a requirement:** Training, shadowing, micro-promotions, and stretch assignments are not extras; they're the job.

- **Stewardship:** Treat people's time, energy, and trust like precious resources—because they are.

- **Community:** Build a team identity that outlasts a shift or a metric; celebrate reliability, not only hero moments.

"Serve first, set the standard second, and systems will start serving everyone." – Heather Williams

A Notable Voice: Robert K. Greenleaf

Robert K. Greenleaf, in his landmark essay *The Servant as Leader*, asked a simple test: *Do those served grow as persons—becoming healthier, wiser, freer, more autonomous, and more likely themselves to become servants?*

His vision wasn't sentimental; it was **operational**. Leadership effectiveness is measured by the growth and well-being of the people entrusted to you—and the community you build together. (See also the summarized characteristics often associated with servant leadership: listening, empathy, healing, awareness, persuasion, conceptualization, foresight, stewardship, commitment to people's growth, and building community.)

Greenleaf (paraphrased): The best test is whether those served grow—and whether the least privileged are helped, or at least not further deprived.

Leaders like **Cheryl Bachelder** (Popeyes) and **Satya Nadella** (Microsoft) have championed people-first turnarounds— prioritizing franchisees and employees' success (Bachelder) and installing empathy as a performance driver (Nadella).

Case Study: Servant Leadership in a Healthcare RCM Team

Context:

A patient billing (RCM) call-center was struggling inconsistent FCR, variable quality scores, rising denials, and creeping turnover. Agents felt over-measured and under- supported.

Servant-Leadership Moves:

1. **Listen, map, remove friction.**

o 1:1 listening sessions asking, *"What slows you down?"*

o Gemba-style call reviews to see where scripts confused rather than clarified.

o Immediate fixes: simplified identity-verification prompts; one-page "Quick Answers" for top five billing scenarios (EOBs, prior auth, financial assistance, payment at time of call, corrected claims).

2. **Protect time and attention.**

o Daily 10-minute huddles: one update, one skill, one shout- out.

o Quiet blocks for deep work on complex cases; camera- optional meetings to reduce fatigue.

3. **Coach growth, not just gaps.**

o Same-day feedback framing: *what worked + one next behavior.*

o Buddy system: pair warm communicators with detail anchors for cross-strength learning.

4. **Advocate upward**

o Secured leadership support for a clean, searchable knowledge base; got billing to fast-track corrected-claim requests from the pod.

o Locked a follow-up SLA so

"owned issues" didn't languish.

5. **Cultivate community.**

o Recognized reliability (clean notes, kept follow-ups, zero- defect days), not only speed.

o Shared "why it matters" stories: how a corrected claim prevented collections, or an EOB explanation kept a patient in care.

Outcomes (within two months):

- **FCR** improved as agents found answers in seconds and owned end-to- end resolutions.

- **QA** rose with fewer reworks—note hygiene and warm handoffs became habit.

- **Patient sentiment** shifted positive: calmer calls, clearer next steps, fewer callbacks.

- **Retention** stabilized as stress decreased, and agents saw a path to growth (micro-promotions, specialty lanes).

Why it worked:

The leader served the team—listened, removed obstacles, tailored roles to strengths, and translated the mission ("keep patients in care") into daily behaviors. As people grew, **the system improved**.

"When you grow your people, they grow your results." - Heather Williams

How to Practice Servant Leadership (Playbook)

- **Start with a Listening Sprint:** 15- minute 1:1s asking three questions:

1. What energizes you here?
2. What drains you here?

3. What one thing would help you serve patients better this week?

- **Make the right way the easy way:** One living knowledge base in plain language; <5-second search.

- **Redesign around strengths:** Assign denial triage to pattern-spotters; EOB explanations to empathic communicators; note standards to detail anchors.

- **Coach in inches:** One behavior, one metric, one week. Keep / tweak / toss.

- **Tell the "why":** Tie each script, checklist, and policy to how it protects the patient.

- **Measure what matters:** Reliability and resolution—clean handoffs, kept follow-ups, reduced rework—not just speed.

- **Advocate relentlessly:** Remove cross- department friction (billing, IT, clinical handoffs) so your team can do meaningful work.

"Servant leadership turns authority into trust, and trust into outcomes." – Heather Williams

Bottom line: Influence built on **service** is influence that lasts. By centering people— listening deeply, aligning work to strengths, and clearing paths—you don't just improve metrics; you build a community capable of **extraordinary** care, one ordinary interaction at a time.

Finding and Growing the Best Talent

Being the best leader doesn't mean you have all the answers; it means you **surround yourself with people who do**—and then build a system where their best work becomes normal. In healthcare operations, I made it my mission to find people with **expertise, empathy, and drive**, and to create an environment where that mix could thrive.

"If you build the relationships, the talent will find you. If it doesn't, you'll find it—and if you can't find it, you'll develop it." -Heather Williams

Relationships First, Résumés Second

The most reliable talent I've hired didn't start with a job posting; it started with a **relationship**—someone we collaborated with, coached, or served alongside. When you invest in people consistently, word spreads.

Your "brand" as a leader becomes, *this is a place where I'll grow and be treated with respect.* That draws strong people in.

Where the best talent came from

- **Internal referrals:** High performers refer to people who share their standards.

- **Former colleagues and vendors:** People who've seen you operate already know your bar.

- **Community partners:** Workforce boards, language programs (like English Under the Arches), local colleges.

- **Alumni network:** Stay close to previous employees who left well; many boomerang back—or send talent your way.

- **Patient-facing excellence:** Kind, composed staff in adjacent departments can be cross-trained into RCM roles.

How relationships turn into hires

- Keep a **warm list** of 10–15 people you'd hire tomorrow; check in quarterly.

- Invite top prospects to **shadow a huddle** or observe a coaching session.

- Offer **30–60 minute "job auditions"** (paid when possible): practice one call scenario or one denial triage.

- Share **real problems** you're solving and ask how they'd approach them— watch their thinking, not just their talking.

"Hire for learning velocity and empathy— then teach the rest."
Heather Williams

What We Looked For (Beyond Skills)

- **Learning velocity:** Do they absorb, apply, and iterate quickly?

- **Empathy under pressure:** Can they calm a caller—and themselves?

- **Judgment in the gray:** Do they know when to ask, escalate, or act?

- **Ownership:** Do they say, "I'll own this and close the loop"?

- **Team lift:** Do they make the people around them better?

Make Talent Come to You (Be a Talent Magnet)

Great people choose places where they can **do great work** without unnecessary friction. That means:

- **Clarity:** One living knowledge base, clear goals, and clean handoffs.

- **Growth path:** A visible ladder (Agent

  $\rightarrow$ Senior $\rightarrow$ QA/Trainer $\rightarrow$ Lead $\rightarrow$ Manager) and a **lattice** for specialists (denials, benefits, financial assistance).

- **Weekly attention:** 15-minute check- ins (What energized you? What drained you? What's the priority this week?).

- **Psychological safety:** It's safe to ask questions, surface risks, and admit mistakes.

- **Recognition:** Reliability (clean notes, kept follow-ups, zero-defect days) gets as much applause as speed.

"Top talent doesn't want ping-pong tables; they want a leader who removes roadblocks."– Heather Williams

Develop What You Can't Find

If the market doesn't offer what you need, build it.

90-Day Development Plan (example)

- **Days 1–30:** Foundations—HIPAA, systems, tone; side-by-side shadowing; top five scenarios; daily micro- coaching.
- **Days 31–60:** Autonomy—handle moderate complexity; warm transfers; note hygiene; weekly strengths-aligned coaching.
- **Days 61–90:** Specialty—choose a lane (EOBs, denials, PA/COB); mentor one new hire; quality >90%.

  On-the-job rituals that accelerate growth

- **10-minute daily practice** on one scenario.
- **Buddy system** (pair a warm communicator with a detail anchor).
- **Same-day QA feedback**: what worked + one next behavior.
- **"Keep / Tweak / Toss"** weekly improvement on one microprocess.

  Mini-Case: Relationships → Talent →Leader

We needed a bilingual agent for complex billing/EOB calls. A former colleague introduced us to a cashier-turned-shift-lead known for her calm under pressure ways. Within 90 days she hit QA >90%, and by six months she was mentoring others in empathy scripting. We didn't "find" a unicorn—we **recognized capacity**, invested attention, and built the runway.

What made it work?

- Relationship-based recruiting (trusted referral).
- Strengths-aligned training (empathy first, complexity second).
- Weekly attention and a clear path to lead a specialty.

Measure What Matters

Track whether your relationship-first, growth- centered approach is working:

- **Time-to-fill** (down)
- **Ramp time** to QA/FCR targets (down)
- **Quality of hire** (QA $\geq$ 90% by day 60)
- **6–12-month retention** (up)
- **Internal mobility** (promotions/role changes)

"Grow your people and your pipeline. One feeds the other." - Heather Williams

Bottom Line

Talent is attracted by **clarity**, **care**, and **credible growth**. Build rich relationships in your community, be the kind of leader who pays attention every week, and design work around strengths. Do that, and the best people will find you—or they'll become the best people because they found *you!*

Promoting Continual Growth

Growth in healthcare isn't optional—it's **survival**. Policies shift, billing rules evolve, payer portals change, technologies update, and patient expectations rise. Your job as a leader is to **guide your team through change** so they adapt quickly **without** losing sight of excellence and compassion.

Externally, that means staying plugged into industry trends and peer networks so you can anticipate change. Internally, it means building a culture where curiosity is normal, learning is constant, and small improvements ship **every week**.

"Change moves whether we like it or not. Growth is choosing to move on purpose." – Heather Williams

Make Growth Inevitable (Build the System Around It)

1) Install Learning Loops (Weekly) – Learn→ Apply → Measure → Share

- **Learn:** 10-minute micro-lesson in huddle (HIPAA refreshers, new payer policy, empathy scripting).
- **Apply:** One tiny behavior change on the floor that same day.
- **Measure:** Track one number (FCR, QA item, seconds saved, reworks avoided).
- **Share:** Post a quick "what worked" note in the knowledge base before the next shift.

2) One Living Knowledge Base

- Plain language, searchable in <5 seconds.
- Single source of truth for top scenarios (EOB explanations, PA rules, COB, corrected claims, financial assistance).
- Timestamp changes and add a 2- sentence "what's new" banner so agents don't guess.

3) Micro–Skill Sprints (2–3 Weeks)

Pick one capability (e.g., denial triage, warm transfers, note hygiene).

- Week 1: baseline + one small standard
- Week 2: practice + peer shadow
- Week 3: lock the win (update KB + QA rubric)

4) Strengths-Aligned Development

Use your weekly 1:1s to place people where they learn fastest:

- Pattern-spotters → denial analytics, benefits verification.
- Empathizers → EOB explanations, financial-navigation calls
- Detail-anchors → note standards, KB upkeep, QA calibration.

5) Visible Growth Paths

Show ladders (Agent → Senior → QA/Trainer→ Lead → Manager) **and** lattices (benefits, denials, FA specialist). Map the skills and the practice reps required for each step so growth feels **achievable**, not abstract.

6) Cadence That Protects Learning

- **Daily:** 10-minute huddle (one update, one skill, one shout-out)
- **Weekly:** Team retro (Keep / Tweak / Toss one micro-process)
- **Monthly:** Calibration lab (listen to 2–3 calls together; one behavior to standardize)
- **Quarterly:** "Level Up" day (cross- train a new lane; refresh HIPAA & payer changes)

Lead the Change (So the Team Can Run It)

When something big shifts—new payer rules, a portal overhaul, revised scripts—use a simple, steady pattern:

1. **Why** – What changed and how it protects patients or speeds resolution.

2. **What** – The exact behaviors/scripts/tools that change

3. **How** – Show the flow live (screenshare + sample calls)

4. **When** – Start date, grace period, and

   how we'll measure success.

5. **Support** – Where to click, who to ping, and office hours for questions

"Name reality, then name a path." – Heather Williams

Connect to the Outside (Bring Back What Matters)

- **Payer roundtables & user groups:** Learn denial trends, portal updates, and PA nuances—translate them to plain-English playbooks for your team.

- **Local workforce partners & colleges:** Build pipelines for bilingual talent and RCM apprenticeships.

- **Peer networks & forums:** Swap micro-standards (scripts, checklists, QA rubrics) that others have already battle-tested.

Rule: Only bring back what you can **teach in 10 minutes** and **measure in a week**.

Mini-Case: The Denial Drop Sprint (6 Weeks)

Problem: Rising denials. Stress up, rework up, patient trust down.

Sprint Plan:

- **Week 1 – Baseline & Map:** Identify top three denial codes; map the exact failure points.
- **Week 2 – One-Page Fix:** Build a quick-answer sheet.
- **Week 3 – Train Small:** 10-minute daily drills on the three scenarios.
- **Week 4 – QA as Coaching:** Same-day feedback on the three items only.
- **Week 5 – Handoff Hygiene:** Standardize warm transfer script to billing leads; require a one-line summary in notes.
- **Week 6 – Lock & Share:** KB updated; celebrate drop in rework and denials; add the new checklist to onboarding.

Results: Denials down double-digits; FCR up; fewer callbacks; calmer patients. No huge overhaul—just **continuous learning packaged in weeks, not quarters**.

What to Measure (So Growth Sticks)

- **Process:** time-to-update knowledge base; % of agents using new note template

- **Quality:** QA item pass rate on the new standard; reworks avoided

- **Outcome:** FCR lift; denial reduction; patient sentiment on clarity and care

- **People:** ramp time to proficiency; 6– 12-month retention; internal mobility

"If you can't see the learning in your numbers, you didn't finish the change." – Heather Williams

Culture Signals That Say "We Grow Here"

- **Leaders learn aloud:** "Here's what I got wrong last week—and what I changed."

- **Questions are welcome:** Office hours, hotlines, and a no-shame policy for asking.

- **Wins are specific:** "Your note saved five minutes for the next rep and spared the patient a retell."

- **Standards evolve:** Yesterday's script can be improved today. That's not instability—that's craftsmanship.

Bottom line: In healthcare, growth is how you stay worthy of the trust patients give you.

Build the rhythms, tools, and relationships that make learning automatic, and your team will find **better, faster, more compassionate** ways to serve—again next week, and the week after that.

The Ripple Effect of Influence

Influence in healthcare leadership isn't confined to the four walls of your office. The way you show up shapes how supervisors show up, how agents speak to patients, and how those patients feel about their care. **Every decision, every conversation, and every example you set sends ripples through the organization**—upstream to executives, downstream to frontline teams, and outward to patients, payers, and the community.

"Leaders set the temperature. Teams set the table. Patients feel the meal." – Heather Williams

How a Leader's Behavior Cascades

- **Tone → Safety:** Calm, curious leadership creates psychological safety. Safe teams surface risks early, fix defects faster, and learn aloud.

- **Clarity → Consistency:** Clear standards (what good looks like) become consistent behaviors on calls, in notes, and in handoffs.

- **Purpose → Pride:** When you connect tasks to patient outcomes, work feels meaningful; people own results rather than comply with rules.

- **Attention → Growth:** Frequent, specific coaching raises capability; capability raises confidence; confidence improves patient experience.

A "One Decision" Ripple Map

(Billing/RCM Example)

Leader decision: Adopt **warm transfers** (no cold handoffs), with a one-sentence summary logged in the note.

- **Supervisors:** Model the script, coach the behavior, recognize good examples in huddles.

- **Agents:** Patients stop repeating their story; anxiety drops; issues resolve faster.

- **Patients:** Sentiment improves; trust rises; follow-ups and care adherence increase.

- **System:** Fewer callbacks, clearer notes for next touch, reduced rework, and denials.

- **Outcomes:** Higher FCR/QA, lower abandon rate and complaints, better collections with less stress.

Mini-Case: Changing Three Words Changed the Month

Before: Agents opened balance calls with,

"This is what you owe."

After: We trained a new opener: **"Here's what your plan paid, what they didn't, and why—then we'll talk options."**

Ripple:

- Patients felt respected and informed (sentiment up).

- Fewer escalations; more successful financial-navigation calls.

- Collections improved with **less** friction because trust went up.

- Agents reported **lower stress** and higher confidence.

  Three words ("paid / didn't / why") reframed the conversation—and the metrics followed.

Make Your Ripples Intentional (Leader Playbook)

- **Model first minutes:** Open meetings the way you want calls opened—clear agenda, purpose, and next steps.

- **Name the "why":** Tie every script or policy change to the patient's experience.

- **Standardize the small stuff:** One living knowledge base; warm-transfer template; note hygiene that saves the next person five minutes.

- **Coach in inches:** One behavior per week, measured and recognized.
- **Shine light on reliability:** Celebrate clean handoffs, kept follow-ups, and zero-defect days—not just speed.

"Your habits become your team's habits. Choose them like patients are listening— because they are." -Heather Williams

How to Measure the Ripples

Link leader behaviors to outcomes you can see:

- **Team health:** 1:1 completion rate, eNPS/pulse, retention (6–12 months).
- **Quality & flow:** QA empathy/accuracy, FCR, AHT driven by clarity (not rush), rework/denial rate.
- **Patient experience:** Post-call sentiment, complaint rate, escalation volume, callback reduction.
- **Financial impact:** Bad debt/charity approvals done correctly, payment- plan uptake, payer reprocess success.

30–60–90 Day Influence Cascade

- **Days 1–30:** Pick one behavior (e.g., warm transfers). Train, coach, and measure it visibly.
- **Days 31–60:** Add one documentation standard (one-sentence summary). QA calibrates to it; celebrate good notes daily.

- **Days 61–90:** Embed a weekly 10- minute huddle ritual (one update, one skill, one shout-out). Publish wins + "why it matters" stories.

When leadership and influence are used intentionally, those ripples **become waves**—of trust, excellence, and impact. Your people feel supported, your patients feel cared for, and your numbers tell the same story: better clarity, fewer errors, calmer calls, and outcomes you can be proud of.

Closing Thought

Leadership isn't about being the most knowledgeable person in the room—it's about being the person who **raises the room**. Your job is to turn individual effort into collective excellence. Influence is the bridge between intention and impact, and it's built from three materials: **trust** (people believe you), **relationships** (people belong with you), and **vision** (people see where you're going and why it matters). When those are in place, an ordinary team becomes an extraordinary force for change—steadily, predictably, together.

"Lead so others can do their best work—then watch the work get better than you imagined." – Heather Williams

How to live this tomorrow (90 seconds):

- **Name reality, then a path:** "This is hard—and here's our first next step."

- **Model the tone you want echoed:** Calm, clear, and patient—especially under pressure.

- **Give frequent, specific attention:** One behavior to keep, one to improve, one resource to help.

- **Connect tasks to purpose:** Tie every script, checklist, and metric to the patient or customer it protects.

- **Celebrate reliability, not just heroics:** Clean handoffs, kept follow- ups, zero-defect days.

Influence compounds in inches: how you open a meeting, how you handle a mistake, how you close a loop. Do those inches well, again tomorrow, and you won't just manage outcomes—you'll **shape a culture** where excellence is the norm and progress are the habit. That's leadership that lasts.

Chapter 6 – Sacrifice and the Invisible Woman

The Cost at Home (and the Ongoing Repair)

Leadership can be rewarding, but it often carries a cost we don't talk about enough: the quiet, persistent sacrifice of your personal life. My highlight reel is full of milestones hit, teams built, and problems solved. But there's a second reel that plays beside it—school plays missed, classroom awards I heard about after the fact, everyday memories that don't replay on command. Those moments don't come back.

I told myself I was doing it for them. And I was. I wanted my children to have opportunities I didn't—security, education, choices. But in leadership—especially in a 24/7 environment like McDonald's and later in healthcare—your success depends on how your team performs, and your team's performance depends on you showing up, no matter what's happening at home. That constant readiness can turn you into **the invisible woman**: visible everywhere except in your own life.

I'm still making up for those sacrifices. That's the truth. Repair is not a weekend project; it's a way of living. Some days it looks like presence—phone down, eyes up, listening with both ears. Some days it looks like apology—no justification, no "but" just ownership. Some days it's planning—putting family on the calendar first, then building work around it. And many days it's patience—allowing time for trust to grow back slowly.

"Providing for your family is love. So is being with them. A life well-led must do both." – Heather Williams

Would I Do It Again?

People ask me if I'd make the same choices, knowing what they cost at home. My answer—selfish or not—is **yes**. I would do it again **for the purpose**: to create stability, to open doors, to break ceilings. But I would do it **differently** in the *how*:

- I would **protect non-negotiables** (red- letter dates, key performances, doctor visits) the same way I protected a launch or an inspection.

- I would **design coverage**—train and trust my team—so leadership didn't always equal personal sacrifice.

- I would **name the tradeoffs out loud** to my family and include them in planning, so no one felt blindsided by my absence.

- I would **measure success at home** with the same seriousness I measured KPIs at work.

It's not either/or. It's both/and—**provision and presence**. The work honored our future; the presence honors our now.

How I'm Making Amends (and How You Can, Too)

1) Truth & Repair Conversations

A simple four-step framework with the people you love:

- **Acknowledge:** "I missed moments that mattered to you."
- **Own:** "That hurt. I'm not excusing it."
- **Ask:** "What would help now? What tradition could we build together?"
- **Commit:** "Here's what I'll protect next month—and how you'll know."

2) Red-Letter Calendar

Put family milestones on the calendar first each quarter. Share it with your team. Build staffing and on-call rotations around it where possible.

3) One-on-One Rituals

Monthly, predictable, and simple: a breakfast date, a walk, a game night. Presence compounds. It doesn't have to be fancy to be meaningful.

4) Legacy Notes

Short letters or voice notes before big days you can't attend: *"What I love about you…*

what I'm proud of... what I'm excited to hear afterward." They become keepsakes that travel farther than your schedule.

5) Boundary Signals

- **Hard stop** one evening per week (no calls, no email).
- **Device basket** during meals.
- **On-call rotation** you design with your team, so leadership is **shared**, not **shouldered**.

6) Measurable Home KPIs (Yes, really.)

- Two protected events/month.
- One undistracted hour, twice a week.
- One new tradition each season.

  Track it for 90 days. If you can measure work, you can measure what matters most.

What I'd Tell My Children Now

I would tell them that ambition was never the opposite of love. It was *because* I loved them that I fought for a different future. I would also tell them that love requires presence— time, attention, unhurried moments. I can't replace what's gone, but I can **honor what is here**. I can choose differently now.

"You can't rewind a childhood, but you can redeem a relationship—one present moment at a time." – Heather Williams

From Invisible to Seen

Buying a dog changed my pace—and my perspective. Caring for a being who needs nothing, but presence and consistency taught me the simplest truth: **showing up is love in motion**. A dog doesn't ask for a promotion or a perfect plan. They ask for eye contact, a calm voice, a walk at their pace, and the certainty that you'll come back. That rhythm softened my edges. It taught me patience, play, and the power of being fully there—no phone, no multitasking, no agenda.

My dogs became **love teachers**:

- **Patience:** They wait at the door until I'm ready, reminding me that timing can be gentle.
- **Forgiveness:** They forget yesterday's missed walk and light up at today's leash.
- **Presence:** They don't care about my title; they care that I'm on the floor, at their level.
- **Joy:** They celebrate ordinary moments like they're holidays—a bowl filled, a sunbeam found, a familiar voice.

"Dogs taught me the math of love: attention multiplied by time equals trust." – Heather Williams

That love for dogs, joined with my love for people, birthed **Making Change Pawsible Inc.** Serving animals who can't speak for themselves helped me become visible to myself again. It re-anchored me in purpose— and it reminded me that love isn't only a feeling; it's a series of choices, repeated daily, for someone else's good.

I can't go back and redo every moment with my children. That truth carries weight. But life gave me a grace I didn't expect **grandchildren**. With them, I practice what the dogs taught me— **quiet presence**. We celebrate small rituals that mean everything: such as walks where I let *them* set the pace, cheering from the sideline. I listen to the whole story, even when it wanders. I memorize their laughter the way my dogs memorize the sound of my keys. I am building **new firsts**—not to replace the old, but to honor the time I have now.

"I don't get a do-over; I get a do-better. And I'm doing better—on purpose." – Heather Williams

This is what I know now: **sacrifice** is part of leadership; **repair** is part of legacy. If you're living in the tension between the two, don't choose shame—choose strategy. Design your leadership so the people you lead at work **and** the people you love at home both get what they need: your excellence and your presence.

How I practice it now:

- **Red-letter family first:** I block grandkid milestones on the calendar before I fill it with meetings.

- **Presence rituals:** One-on-one time.

- **Small, steady service:** Daily dog care as a spiritual practice— walks, meals, play—because consistency is love you can see.

- **Honest conversations:** "I missed things before. I'm here for this." And then I prove it.

Would I do it all again? **Yes**—for the purpose, for the doors it opened, for the future it built. But I'd do it with **better boundaries, clearer conversations, and a calendar that proves who I love**. Provision builds our tomorrow; presence builds our today. My dogs taught me how to slow down enough to love in real time. My grandchildren give me a fresh place to pour that love.

"Love isn't loud. It shows up, on time, again tomorrow." – Heather Williams

I choose both now—**purpose and presence**. And I measure my days less by what I produced and more by who felt seen because I was there.

Losing Your Way to Find It Again

There came a point when I didn't even realize how invisible I'd become. I was efficient, reliable, "on"—and oddly absent from my own life. I answered every alert and missed the quiet signals: the fatigue that didn't lift, the dinners eaten standing up, the way weekends felt like staging areas for Monday. I wasn't unhappy; I was **unnoticed**—mostly by me.

Then I bought a dog—or rather, my grandson picked one for me. He chose a fluffy brown doodle, looked up with that serious little face, and said, "His name is Pretzel." Pretzel is three years old now—sixty pounds of joy, stubbornness, and steady love. From day one he reorganized my house and my calendar: morning walks that forced me to breathe, evening play that forced me to put the phone down, soft eyes that asked for presence, not performance. He didn't care about titles or timelines. He cared that I showed up. Pretzel became the face of **Making Change Pawsible**. Pretzel makes the mission visible: no speeches, just warmth. Everyone remembers his name.

Me? I'm the girl in the background. Pretzel gets the spotlight; I keep the bowls filled. That balance feels right. He is the invitation; I am the follow-through. Together we practice what this book has taught: Mindset every morning, I'm Possible in every problem, respect for the "mediocre" middle where systems are built, and the extraordinary found in ordinary acts. My grandson chose a dog; the dog helped choose our mission; and the mission keeps choosing us—one full bowl, one wagging tail, one family at a time.

It sounds simple, almost trivial, but that decision changed my rhythm. Suddenly, there was a living clock in my home whose needs didn't care about my inbox—morning light, fresh water, a walk, a real pause. The leash became a line back to myself. Step outside.

Breathe air that isn't recirculated. Watch how a body relaxes when the world is not a meeting. Notice how joy appears for no reason at all.

With a dog, presence isn't optional; it's how the relationship works. They read your posture before your words, your tone before your plan. I learned to soften my shoulders, lower my voice, and mean it. Without realizing it, I was practicing **M·I·M·E**—communicating through movement and intention, not speeches. That practice spilled back into leadership: fewer long announcements, more clear signals; less pressure, more steadiness; a team that sensed calm because I carried it.

Daily care became daily anchors: food at regular times, a lap around the block at dusk, ten minutes on the floor with a tennis ball.

These weren't to-do items. They were **recalibrations**. Routine turned into ritual, and ritual turned into a way home to me. I started making different choices outside the leash, too—blocking short, untouchable windows on my calendar, finishing the day with a real ending, leaving one inch of margin around the edges of each week.

"Sometimes the fastest way back to yourself is a slower creature who refuses to be rushed." – Heather Williams

What I learned walking beside that animal is that recovery doesn't need a grand plan; it needs **small consistencies**. The body remembers before the mind agrees. You arrive back at your life in footsteps, not leaps—five quiet minutes at dawn, a longer exhale before you reply, one less promises you can't keep.

Slowly, the metrics you've used to measure yourself—output, speed, availability—begin to share space with gentler ones: presence, pace, peace.

And the surprising part? The work improved. Teams take their cue from a leader's nervous system. When I carried less frenzy, they carried more focus. When I modeled boundaries, they believed they were allowed to have them. The business didn't suffer; it steadied.

A simple reset you can try:

- **Two-ground rule (60 seconds):** Put both feet flat on the floor, both hands still on your lap, and breathe out longer than you breathe in— four rounds. Then speak. Your tone will do more than your words ever could.

- **Leash logic (10 minutes):** Step outside with no phone. Walk one block at an unhurried pace. Name three things you can see, two you can hear, one you can feel. Return different.

I didn't find my way with a grand epiphany. I found it by caring for a being who asked nothing of me but presence—and in answering that ask, I relearned how to be present for myself.

From Invisible to Visible Again

That love for dogs, combined with my lifelong passion for people, sparked something bigger: **Making Change Pawsible Inc.**—a nonprofit dedicated to feeding dogs in need. It began with one simple conviction: no dog should go hungry because their human is going through a hard season.

It wasn't just about the dogs. It was about **reclaiming visibility** in my own life. The foundation gave me a way to connect **purpose to passion**—to give in a way that filled my soul instead of draining it. I found myself again in the ordinary acts of service: lifting a bag of food into a trunk, kneeling to meet a nervous pup eye to eye. Small actions, done on purpose, stitched me back into the present.

"We feed dogs, but what we're really serving is dignity—on both ends of the leash." – Heather Williams

Making Change Pawsible: Purpose with Paws

We designed the mission to remove simple barriers with simple solutions:

- **Food Security for Dogs:** Regular distribution of dog food through pop- up events and partner pantries so families don't have to choose between groceries and kibble.
- **Bridge Support:** Short-term assistance (a month or two of food) while a family stabilizes after job loss, illness, or housing transition.
- **Compassion First:** No shaming, no interrogations—just help, information, and a smile.

Every bag of food is more than nutrition; it's a message: *You're not alone. Your dog matters. You matter.*

How the Work Made Me Visible

Service changed **how** I showed up:

- **Rhythm over rush:** Distribution days set a pace I could feel in my body— present, steady, human.

- **Attention over achievement:** Success was measured in tails wagging and shoulders relaxing, not dashboards and deadlines.

- **Community over control:** Donors, and partner orgs taught me to lead by convening—not commanding.

- **Story over stats:** I still love metrics but faces and names became my first indicators of impact.

I realized that visibility isn't crowd noise or public credit; it's **alignment**. When your values and your actions match, you feel seen—even if it's just by the dog in front of you and the person who loves them.

One Story That Stays with Me

A mother raising two kids came to a distribution with a leash wrapped around her wrist and worry wrapped around her face.

Rent had gone up, hours at work had gone down, and her dog was the last piece of continuity in the house. We loaded a month of food into her trunk and set a reminder to check in. Her relief was immediate and quiet. "Now we can keep him," she whispered, "and the kids can sleep."

That's what a bag of food can do: it keeps a family intact and a memory alive. Ordinary things, extraordinary impact.

You Can't Go Back—But You Can Build Forward

The hardest truth remains **you can't get back what you've lost.** The moments I missed with my children will always be missed moments. But regret isn't a strategy. **Presence is.** You can decide to show up differently now.

How I practice that decision:

- **Red-letter presence:** Family milestones go on the calendar first—then work fits around them.
- **Hands-free rituals:** Phone facedown when I'm with loved ones; attention is the new luxury.
- **Service as a sabbath:** Foundation work as a weekly reset—slowing down to speed up the right things.
- **Teach what I wish I'd known:** Coaching my team (and my grandkids) that provision and presence aren't rivals—they're partners.

"I can't rewrite yesterday, but I can write today on purpose." – Heather Williams

Why Dogs—Why Now

People sometimes ask, "Why dogs?" Because love often **returns** through the door you can still walk through. I couldn't redo the past, but I could **add goodness to the present**—and feeding dogs turned out to be a direct line to human hearts. Dogs keep people grounded, motivated, and less alone. When we remove the fear of 'Can I feed my dog this week?' We remove one more reason to give up.

That's how I became visible again—to my community, to my family, and most importantly, to myself. The work isn't flashy, but it is faithful. It lets me serve with the same intensity I brought to my career—only now, the scoreboard is simpler: full bowls, softer shoulders, steadier homes.

Bottom line: You can't go back. But you can **build forward**—with purpose, with presence, and with a love that shows up in ways that can be felt. For me, that's a leash in one hand and a calendar that proves who I love in the other.

Finding Balance Moving Forward

The lesson for me was simple but profound: **balance doesn't happen—it's built.** You architect it like any reliable system, then you guard it, protect it, and—on the hard weeks— fight for it. Work will always be demanding. Leadership will always ask for sacrifice. But sacrifice should not mean **self-erasure**.

Staying visible to yourself, to your loved ones, and to what matters most doesn't dilute your leadership—it **deepens** it.

"Balance is a design choice you prove with your calendar." – Heather Williams

Build It Like a System (Audit → Architect→ Align)

1) Audit (30 minutes):

- List your *real* weekly load (work blocks, commute, on-call, family care, recovery time).
- Circle what gives energy; underline what drains it.
- Star the moments that must be protected (kids' events, health, quiet time).

2) Architect (45 minutes):

- Place **red-letter non-negotiables** first (family milestones, personal health anchors).
- Layer work around them: focus blocks, huddles, on-call rotations, meeting caps.
- Create a **coverage map** so the team can run without you (names, escalation flow, SLAs).

3) Align (15 minutes):

- Share the plan with your team (what's protected, how to reach you, who covers).
- Share it with family (what's flexible, what's not, and when you'll make it up if needed).

Guardrails That Hold (Personal, Team, Family)

Personal guardrails

- **First 20 / Last 20:** no email, no work chat; use for prep and wind-down.
- **Two device-free hours** each week with family or self.
- **Micro-sabbaths:** two 10-minute pauses per day (walk, breathwork, prayer, journaling).

Team guardrails

- **Office hours** for ad-hoc questions (reduces after-hours pings).
- **On-call rotation** with crystal-clear criteria for true emergencies.
- **Decision ladders:** what agents own, what leads decide, what escalates to you.

Family guardrails

- **Red-letter calendar** published at the start of each month.

- **One standing ritual** per person (breakfast date, park walk, game night).

- **Repair script** for unavoidable misses:

○ *Acknowledge* ("I missed what mattered")

○ *Own* ("No excuses")

○ *Ask* ("What would help now?")

○ *Commit* (specific make-up plan)

"Say 'no' to work you don't need so you can say 'yes' to the people who do." – Heather Williams

Delegate, Don't Disappear (Coverage You Can Trust)

- **If-not-me, then-who?** Create a two- name backup for each recurring task.

- **Shadow → share → shift:** have a teammate observe, co-own for two cycles, then lead it.

- **Document the "gold path":** one-page playbooks (what good looks like, who to ping, how to close the loop).

Result: You're not the bottleneck. The system gets stronger, and balance becomes sustainable.

Energy Management (Not Just Time Management)

- **3S daily baseline: Sleep** (7+), **Steps** (20–30 minutes), **Stillness** (5–10 minutes).

- **Match work to your peak:** Do judgment-heavy tasks in your best energy window.

- **Leave margin:** Keep 10–15% of your week unscheduled for surprises. Protect it.

Visibility Rituals (So Balance Doesn't Fade)

- **Weekly 1:1 with yourself (15 minutes):** What mattered? What drained? What changes next week?

- **Family huddle (10 minutes, Sundays):** Top moments, key events, one fun plan.

- **Team retro (15 minutes, Fridays):** Keep / Tweak / Toss one micro-process to make next week easier.

Metrics That Matter (Your Life Dashboard)

- **Home KPIs:** two protected events/month; two device-free hours/week; one new tradition/season.

- **Work health:** 1:1 completion rate, vacation taken, on-call escalation quality.

- **Early warnings:** you're skipping meals, snapping in meetings, or "forgetting" wins—time to rebalance.

"If you don't measure it, you'll drift from it." -Heather Williams

Quarterly Reset (Renegotiate, Realign, Refresh)

Every 90 days:

- Re-audit your calendar.

- Renegotiate one commitment that no longer fits.

- Refresh one ritual that's gone stale.

- Reaffirm the red letters.

Bottom Line

Balance is not a luxury—**it's leadership infrastructure**. When you design it, guard it, and adjust it in real time, you don't just feel better—you **perform** better. Your team reads your steadiness. Your family feels your presence. And you stop trading today's relationships for tomorrow's results.

"Build the life you won't need a break from— and lead from there."
– Heather Williams

Closing Thought

Sacrifice is part of the journey—but so is recovery. You may lose your way for a season, trading presence for performance and connection for constant availability. There is always a way back. It rarely arrives as a grand moment; it comes as small, repeatable choices: a boundary you keep, a walk you don't cancel, a conversation you finish without looking at your phone.

For me, that path was paved with paw prints. Caring for my dogs taught me a simpler math of love—show up, on time, again tomorrow. It reminded me that visibility isn't fame or applause; it's alignment. It's when what you value and how you live finally match. You don't need to be seen by everyone—you need to **see yourself** clearly enough to choose the next right step, and then another.

"Recovery is just presence, repeated." –Heather Williams

If you're coming back from a season of sacrifice, start small:

- Name one person (or pup) you'll show up for this week.

- Protect one hour that belongs to you and the people you love.

- Keep one promise to yourself, then keep it again tomorrow.

That's how you return—quietly, steadily, on purpose—until your life looks like you again.

Personal Life Is Not a Luxury (Anymore)

Balance is not something you stumble upon— it's something you consciously create.

After years of being the "invisible woman," consumed by work demands and constant responsibility, I realized that reclaiming my personal life wasn't just about taking time off. It was about intentionally building a life outside of work that felt meaningful, connected, and fulfilling.

"Don't get so busy making a living that you forget to make a life."
— Dolly Parton

Those words hit me deeply because for so long, I was guilty of doing exactly that.

I grew up in a time—and in workplaces— where the unspoken rule was clear: **a personal life is a luxury**. You earned it by outperforming, by outlasting, by being the one who stayed when others went home.

Weekends were rewards, not rights. Vacations were proof you'd "paid your dues." The message was simple: *your value equals your output*.

That mindset forged grit and results—but it also extracted a quiet tax: missed milestones, shortened tempers, and a constant feeling that rest had to be justified. I wore productivity like armor and called it pride. Looking back, I can admit it: **I treated presence like a prize to be won, not a need to be honored**.

Then the world shifted.

As COVID approached—and certainly after it arrived—the conversation changed. We saw how quickly life could tilt. We learned, painfully, that caregiving isn't a side gig, that health isn't guaranteed, and that humans cannot run on adrenaline forever. Remote work blurred lines, essential work stretched nerves, and suddenly "well-being" wasn't fluffy HR language—it was **operational reality**. Organizations started naming burnout. Leaders were asked to lead with empathy, not just efficiency. Families needed flexibility, not just a paycheck. We discovered what was always true: **a personal life isn't indulgence—it's infrastructure**.

Here's what I know now: **Personal life is not a luxury to be earned after excellence; it's the fuel that makes excellence sustainable.** When I protect what matters at home, I show up steadier at work. When I'm present with the people I love, I lead with more patience, clarity, and courage.

"Presence is not a perk. It's part of the job— if the job is your life."
– Heather Williams

The Shift I Made (And You Can, Too)

- **From permission to priority:** I stopped waiting to "deserve" time and started scheduling it first.

- **From hiding to naming** I told my team which family moments were red- letter—and invited them to do the same.

- **From constant availability to clear availability:** Office hours, on-call rotations, and a simple rule: true emergencies only.

- **From hustle as identity to craft as practice:** I still work hard, but now excellence is about **quality + humanity**, not just hours logged.

A Simple Reclaim Plan (Start This Week)

- **Anchor one ritual** you never skip (family dinner, a walk, a call to someone you love).

- **Protect one hour** on your calendar— no email, no chat, no guilt.

- **Say one honest sentence** to your team: "Here's what I'm protecting and how to reach me if it truly can't wait."

- **Define one measure of 'life health'** (two device-free hours/week, two family events/month). Track it like a KPI.

The "good old days" taught me discipline. The last few years taught me discernment. I keep the discipline—I lose the denial. I still believe in high standards, but I also believe in **high stewardship** of the life that makes those standards possible.

Personal life isn't something you get **after** success. It's something you build **so** success doesn't cost you the people and the peace you're working for in the first place.

Small Actions, Big Shifts

Reclaiming your personal life doesn't require grand gestures like quitting your job or moving to a remote island. It begins with **small, deliberate actions**—the kind that fit into real days and create real change.

- **Block sacred time**

   Set aside hours each week that are completely off-limits for work. Put them on the calendar like an unbreakable meeting with yourself or your loved ones—and share those blocks with your team so expectations are clear.

   Example: Wednesdays 6–8pm = family dinner; Sundays 10–11am = weekly reset (planning, reflection, no devices).

   Be present in your moments. Presence isn't accidental; it's designed. Whether it's dinner with family or a walk with your dog, put your phone in a drawer and give the moment your full attention.

Micro-habit: The **2-minute off- ramp**—before you enter the house, sit in the car, breathe out longer than you breathe in (4 rounds), set an intention: *"I'm arriving as the calm one."*

- **Reconnect with old passions**

  Pick up a hobby you abandoned or try something new you've always been curious about. You're not required to be "good" at it—only engaged.

  Ideas: 15 minutes of journaling before bed, a Saturday morning nature walk, a beginner's language app with your grandkids, or a simple volunteer task for Making Change Pawsible.

- **Say "no" without guilt**

  Protect your personal time by recognizing that every "yes" to after-hours work is a "no" to something else important.

  Boundary scripts:

  o "I'm offline at 6pm; I'll jump on this at 7am."

  o "I can do A or B by Friday— your call."

  o "I'm at a family commitment then; here are two alternate times."

"The key is not to prioritize what's on your schedule, but to schedule your priorities." — Stephen Covey

Make It Practical (Tools & Rituals)

- **Red-letter calendar:** Put family events, health appointments, and grandkid activities on the calendar first each month. Build work around those anchors.
- **Device baskets:** Phones go in the basket during meals and one hour before bed.
- **First 20 / Last 20:** No email or work chat during the first and last 20 minutes of your day—use that time for centering (coffee, prayer, stretching, gratitude).
- **The one-inch rule:** Improve one tiny thing today (rewrite a sticky note, prep tomorrow's breakfast, lay out dog- walk gear). Small inches add up.

"Peace is planned. Put it on the calendar or it won't exist." – Heather Williams

Scripts for Common Moments

- **After-hours ping:** "I'm off for the evening. If it's urgent-urgent, call; otherwise, I'll respond in the morning."
- **Weekend request:** "I protect weekends for family. I'll tackle this first thing Monday with fresh eyes."
- **Family ask you'd normally skip:**

"Yes. Put it on the calendar—I'm there." *(Then protect it like a board meeting.)*

A Simple 30-Day Reclaim Plan Week 1 – Protect & Prepare

- Block two sacred hours.
- Start First 20 / Last 20.

Week 2 – Presence & Play

- Add a weekly ritual (walk with your dog at sunset; Sunday with grandkids).
- Try one 15-minute passion session (reading, sketching, crafting).

Week 3 – Boundaries & Backup

- Use one boundary script.
- Delegate one task at work and document the "gold path" so it runs without you.

Week 4 – Review & Renew

- What worked? Keep it.
- What sputtered? Tweak it.
- What drained you? Toss it—or renegotiate it.

Measure it like it matters:

- Device-free hours/week

- Protected events kept/month.

- One joy ritual completed/week.

- Stress rating (quick 1–10 each Friday)

For the Dog Lovers (Presence You Can Feel)

- **Leash logic (10 minutes):** Walk without your phone. Let the dog set the pace. Name three things you see, two you hear, one you feel.

- **Consistency = care:** Same feeding times, same bedtime routine. Predictability is love in action—for them and for you.

"Small acts done on purpose turn into a life you recognize." – Heather Williams

Bottom line: Don't wait for a life overhaul. Choose one tiny behavior today, repeat it tomorrow, and let the inches compound. Small actions create big shifts—especially when you protect them with your calendar and your voice.

Giving Back to the Community (with Making Change Pawsible)

For me, one of the most rewarding ways to reclaim life was giving back. Community service became my anchor—a way to connect with people, make an impact, and rediscover purpose outside of titles and deadlines.

Through **Making Change Pawsible Inc.**, I found a mission simple enough to act on and powerful enough to matter: **no dog goes hungry**.

"When you pour into your community, you refill your own spirit in ways a paycheck never could." – Heather Williams

Why Feeding Dogs Matters (and Helps People)

Dogs are family. When a household hits a rough patch—job loss, illness, housing transitions—pet food is often the first "luxury" cut. Food support prevents forced surrenders, keeps families intact, and lowers shelter intake. Just as importantly, it eases the emotional load for children, seniors, veterans, and anyone for whom a dog is daily comfort and companionship.

Impact flywheel: Full bowls → calmer homes → fewer surrenders → less shelter strain → stronger communities.

What We Do (Programs You Can Replicate Locally)

- **Bridge Bags:** 30–60 days of food for households facing a temporary crisis (job change, medical issue, homelessness).

- **Foster Food Bridge:** Food support for short-term fosters so cost doesn't block a "yes."

- **Paws & Learn:** Quick lessons on canine nutrition, budgeting for pets, and local low-cost resources—printed in English/Spanish at events.

- **Crisis Response:** Rapid deployments to the homeless community providing them with food for their dogs.

"We feed dogs, but what we're really serving is dignity—on both ends of the leash." - Heather Williams

How It Works (Simple, Repeatable, Scalable)

1. **Source:** Donations + bulk purchases when needed.
2. **Schedule:** A predictable quarterly cadence.
3. **Setup:** Tables, signage, and a warm welcome.
4. **Safeguards:** Basic screening to estimate need (no heavy paperwork), pet-safe food handling, and respectful privacy.
5. **Follow-up:** Short check-ins after distribution.

How to Help (Pick One and Start)

- **Donate:** One-time or monthly gifts (even small amounts stabilize inventory).

- **Host a Drive:** Ask your school, gym, or workplace to collect unopened dog food.

- **Match & Multiply:** Set up payroll giving or corporate match programs.

- **Spread the Word:** Share resources with neighbors; post events and needs on social.

- **Partner:** If you run a clinic, shelter, or community org, coordinate calendars so families can access multiple supports in one stop.

Pro tip: Make it social—invite a friend, your team, or your grandkids. Service becomes a shared memory.

What We Measure (Because Impact Should Be Visible)

- **Dogs fed** per month / per quarter.
- **Households served** and % returning vs. stabilized.

Numbers tell the story on a scale; faces and names keep us human.

Giving back is how I found my balance again. **Making Change Pawsible** isn't just about food; it's about **belonging**—for families under pressure, for neighbors who want to help, and for anyone who needs proof that ordinary people can do extraordinary good.

The Ripple Effect of Personal Balance

When you create space for your personal life, it's not just you who benefits. Your family gets a more present you. Your friends get a more engaged you. Even your team gets a leader who is more energized, creative, and resilient. Balance is not time *away* from leadership; it's the energy that makes leadership sustainable.

"A balanced leader leads better, because they lead from a place of wholeness, not depletion." – Heather Williams

What Changes When You're Balanced

At home

- Conversations are longer, kinder, and less transactional.

- Small rituals (dinner, walks, game nights) become anchors that build trust.

- Repair is faster because patience comes easier.

With friends

- You have margin to show up— birthdays, texts returned, a quick coffee that resets a week.

- You're less performative, more real; relationships deepen.

At work (especially in healthcare/RCM)

- **Better decisions:** Rested leaders choose clarity over urgency; fewer "fire drills," more steady execution.

- **Calmer culture:** Your tone sets psychological safety; teams surface issues earlier and fix them faster.

- **Stronger results:** Consistent energy leads to consistent coaching— QA rises, rework drops, patients feel seen.

"Your nervous system is a leadership tool. Calm is contagious." – Heather Williams

Mini-Case: Balance → Better

Outcomes (8 Weeks)

Starting point: Leader answering pings at all hours; team anxious, QA uneven, FCR stuck. **Shifts made:**

- 10-minute daily huddles (one update, one skill, one shout-out).

- Friday 15-minute retro (Keep/Tweak/Toss one micro- process).

Ripples observed:

- Leader calmer; meetings shorter and clearer.

- Team escalations fell; QA +6 points; FCR +7 points.

- Patient sentiment improved (fewer callbacks, clearer next steps). Balance didn't slow the work—it **stabilized** it.

Practices That Create Positive Ripples

- **Red-letter first:** Put family milestones and personal health on your calendar before work blocks. Share them with your team (model the norm).

- **First 20 / Last 20:** No email or chat the first and last 20 minutes of your day; use that time to center and to close with intention.

- **Boundary scripts:**

o "I'm offline after 7pm; if it's urgent-urgent, call. Otherwise, I'll handle it at 8am."

o "I can deliver A by Friday or B by Thursday—your call."

- **Energy audits:** Weekly check-in: What gave energy? What drained it? What do I change next week?

- **Delegate with design:** Shadow → share → shift ownership; create one-page "gold paths" so work runs without you.

How to Measure the Ripple (So It Sticks)

- **Home:** two device-free hours/week; two protected events/month; one ritual sustained 4+ weeks.

- **Team:** 1:1 completion rate; QA trend; FCR trend; escalations per one hundred calls.

- **Self:** sleep hours, "stress score" (1–10) every Friday, days you actually ended on time.

"If you want different outcomes, change the inputs—especially your rest and your rituals." – Heather Williams

30/60/90: Balance Cascade Plan

- **Days 1–30:** Protect two personal blocks/week; install daily 10-minute huddles; turn on on-call rotation.

- **Days 31–60:** Add Friday retro; publish a one-page knowledge quick-answers; track two metrics (QA + FCR).

- **Days 61–90:** Delegate one recurring task permanently; add a monthly Level-Up training; lock the wins into SOPs.

Bottom line: Personal balance is not separate from performance—it **powers** it. Build it, guard it, and your family, friends, and team will all feel the difference. The work gets clearer. The culture gets kinder. The results got better.

Practical Actions to Start Today

1. **Community Hour** – Dedicate one hour per week to a cause that matters to you.

2. **Mindful Start** – Begin your day with a ritual (meditation, journaling, gratitude list) before checking your phone.

3. **Monthly "Life Check"** – Once a month, review how much time you spent on things that truly matter. Adjust accordingly.

4. **Digital Boundaries** – Set a "no work email" rule after a certain time in the evening.

5. **Celebrate Small Wins** – Acknowledge progress in reclaiming your personal life, even if it's as simple as leaving work on time twice this week.

Closing Thought

Reclaiming your personal life isn't about doing less—it's about doing **more of what matters**. It's the shift from busyness to **purpose**, from constant availability to **intentional presence**. When you balance service to others with service to yourself, you don't dilute your impact—you **deepen** it.

Your work becomes clearer, your relationships grow richer, and your days feel like they belong to you again.

Think of balance as architecture, not accident:

- **Blueprint = values.** Name what matters most so your time has a plan.

- **Foundation = health.** Sleep, movement, stillness—without these, everything cracks.

- **Load-bearing walls = relationships.** Protect the people who hold up your life.

- **Beams = boundaries.** Strong "yes" and honest "no" keep the structure sound.

- **Windows = perspective.** Step back to see the whole house, not just one room.

- **Inspections = reviews.** Weekly check- ins to repair, realign, and renew. A simple micro-blueprint you can start today:

1. **Choose one priority** you'll honor this week (family dinner, a walk, a call).

2. **Set one boundary** that protects it (when you're reachable—and when you aren't).

3. **Install one ritual** that refuels you (ten quiet minutes, every day).

"Balance is not found—it's built. And you are the architect." – Heather Williams

Build it piece by piece. Protect it like it matters—because it does. And watch how a life designed around what you value most becomes not just **productive**, but **deeply fulfilling**.

Chapter 8 – Finding Purpose Beyond Self (Making Change Pawsible)

True purpose often reveals itself when we shift our focus from what we can achieve for ourselves to what we can give to others. For me, that shift arrived on four paws, with a wagging tail and an unspoken promise: **no dog under my watch would go hungry**. That promise became *Making Change Pawsible Inc.*, a simple idea with a profound impact— feed the dogs, steady the home, strengthen the community.

"We fill bowls, but what we're really serving is stability, dignity, and hope—on both ends of the leash." -Heather Williams

Why Dogs? Why Now?

Dogs are family. In tough seasons—job loss, illness, housing transitions—pet food is often the first "extra" cut from a strained budget.

That creates a heartbreaking cascade: empty bowls → pet health declines → forced surrenders → children and seniors lose their most reliable source of comfort. One bag of food can interrupt that entire chain.

What a full bowl does:

- Keeps families together.

- Reduces shelter intake and community strain.

- Lowers stress in households already stretched thin.

- Preserves the healing bond between humans and animals.

Purpose with Paws: The MCP Model

Our mission is direct and practical. We designed programs anyone can understand— and replicate:

- **Bridge Bags:** 30–60 days of food during short-term crises (layoffs, medical treatment, relocation).

- **Foster Food Bridge:** Food support to remove cost as a barrier for short-term fosters.

- **Paws & Learn:** One-page handouts on nutrition basics, budgeting for pets, and low-cost care.

Operations in plain language: Source (drives + retail partners) → Schedule (predictable monthlies) → Set up (tables & signage) → Safeguards (pet-safe handling, simple screening, privacy) → Follow-up (friendly check-ins, referrals).

What My Career Taught Me

My years in fast food and healthcare trained me to build systems that *work*—under pressure, at scale, with compassion.

- **Forecasting & flow:** Predict demand by location and season; pre-stage inventory.

- **Quality & consistency:** Simple SOPs for intake and tracking so every event feels organized and respectful.

- **Compliance mindset:** Basic safety protocols, privacy on intake, and transparent reporting to donors and partners.

- **Human-centered service:** "Warm handoffs" to clinics or shelters; clear next steps; phone follow-ups that close the loop.

"Excellence is ordinary work done on purpose—again tomorrow."
– Heather Williams

How We Measure Impact (Because Accountability Matters)

- **Dogs fed** per month / quarter.

- **Households served** and % that stabilized within three months.

- **Surrenders prevented** (self-reported)

Numbers tell scale; **names and faces** keep us honest.

How You Can Help (Start Small, Start Now)

- **Donate** monthly—even modest gifts stabilize inventory.
- **Sponsor a month** in honor of a person or pup you love.
- **Partner** if you're a clinic, shelter, school, or pantry—let's co-locate services.
- **Share the word**—someone in your circle needs this resource.

Website: makingchangepawsible.org

If You Want to Start Your Own

"Micro-Mission"

Use *M·I·M·E* to begin:

- **Mindset:** Start where you are; do for one family what you wish you could do for many.
- **I'm Possible:** Don't wait for perfect funding.
- **Mediocrity as a stage:** Early hiccups are training, not failure. Iterate.
- **Extraordinary in the ordinary:** One consistent event turns into community trust.

The Heart Behind the Work

I can't undo the moments I missed earlier in my life, but I can *add* moments of meaning now—visible, tangible moments that make life better for others. My dogs taught me presence. This mission taught me **purpose beyond self**. It's not loud work; it's faithful work. And it's how I keep choosing a life that aligns with what I value most.

"You don't have to change the whole world; change the part of it you can reach." – Heather Williams

Purpose begins where self-focus ends. For me, it began with a leash, a list of families to call, and a trunk full of dog food. Small actions, done consistently, will carry you farther than grand intentions ever could. Feed one bowl.

Make one call. Host one pop-up. That's how change becomes **pawsible**.

The Birth of Making Change Pawsible

After years of devoting myself to career and leadership, I realized my success felt incomplete without service. I wanted to build something that lived beyond boardrooms and deadlines—something that mattered in the quiet corners of life where no cameras are rolling and no titles matter. Purpose, I learned, isn't proven by what you earn; it's revealed by what you give.

That's where **Making Change Pawsible Inc.** began—not with a strategic plan, but with a look into my own dog's eyes. Safety. Trust. A full bowl and a steady hand. I thought about how many families were doing everything right and still struggling—choosing between groceries and kibble, rent and vet bills, a child's needs, and a dog's meal. I didn't want to analyze that problem from afar. I wanted to put food into bowls. So, I made a promise to myself: **under my watch, no dog would go hungry if I could help it.**

"We fill bowls, but what we're really serving is stability and dignity—on both ends of the leash." – Heather Williams

Building the Mission (One Practical Piece at a Time)

My operations background kicked in. I sketched the **simplest possible system** that would scale:

- **Sourcing:** Pet-food drives, local retail partners, and small grants.
- **Storage & Safety:** Clean, dry storage with rotation by date; sealed bags; safe handling.
- **Distribution:** Monthly "Pet Pantry Pop-Ups" at community hubs.
- **Access:** "Bridge Bags" (30–60 days of food) for families in transition—no heavy paperwork, just basic screening, and a warm conversation.

Why "Pawsible"?

The name is a nod to the heartbeat of this book: **I'm Possible.** We added paws because the mission sits right at the intersection of compassion and action. *Pawsible* is a reminder that small, consistent efforts—one bag, one call, one pop-up—create outsized change. We didn't wait for perfection. We started with possible.

Values We Refused to Compromise

- **Dignity First:** No shaming. No interrogations. Everyone is greeted, helped, and thanked.

- **Simplicity Always:** Clear process. Short lines. Friendly follow-ups.

- **Transparency:** Track what we distribute and where; share outcomes with partners and donors.

- **Partnership Over Pride:** Work with pantries, schools, clinics, and shelters; co-locate services whenever we can.

- **Sustainability:** Build what we can reliably repeat—month after month.

"Excellence is ordinary work done on purpose—again tomorrow."– Heather Williams

Why Feeding Dogs Matters

Some might ask, "With so many human needs in the world, why focus on dogs?"

Because hunger and neglect don't discriminate—and because helping dogs helps people, too. When a family can keep a beloved pet fed, they're more likely to stay stable, avoid heartbreaking surrenders, and maintain the comfort and routine that pets bring—especially for seniors, veterans, and children. A month of dog food can prevent months of emotional stress and costly shelter intake. In other words, a full bowl doesn't just nourish an animal; it preserves a bond, steadies a household, and strengthens the community around it. Dogs are loyal, loving beings who give everything they have to their humans. When hardship hits—job loss, illness, housing transition—pet food is often the first "non-essential" cut. That forces impossible choices: keep the lights on or keep the dog fed; pay the co-pay or buy kibble. A full bowl does more than fill a stomach. It **protects a bond**, prevents surrender, and steadies a home.

The human–animal bond is real care.

- **Mental health:** Pets lower stress and loneliness. For many seniors, veterans, and kids, a dog is daily comfort and routine.
- **Motivation:** Walking, feeding, and caring for a dog keeps people moving, connected, and hopeful during hard seasons.
- **Stability for children:** When everything else changes, a familiar dog helps kids feel safe.

Keeping families together

- **Prevents surrenders:** Food support stops the heartbreaking pipeline to shelters, where space is limited and outcomes are uncertain.
- **Reduces crisis churn:** Families who can keep their pets are less likely to uproot or enter systems already under strain.
- **Supports survivors:** For people living in unsafe situations, knowing a pet will be fed (and can stay) removes one more barrier to getting help.

Community impact (quiet, practical, powerful)

- **Lower shelter load:** Fewer intake spikes mean staff can focus on animals truly in crisis.

- **Public health & safety:** Well-fed dogs are healthier, less likely to roam, and more likely to stay current on basic care when budgets aren't stretched.
- **Cost-effective prevention:** A month of food is often cheaper than the downstream costs of intake, boarding, and rehoming.

Who benefits most?

- **Seniors on fixed incomes** would sooner skip meals than short their pet.
- **Families in transition** (layoffs, medical treatment, temporary housing).
- **Students and single parents**

  balancing rent, books, and groceries.
- **Unhoused neighbors** for whom a dog is protection and companionship.

What one bowl really buys

- **Dignity** for people who love their pets and just need a bridge.
- **Health** through consistent nutrition and fewer stress behaviors.
- **Hope**—the belief that tomorrow can be managed.

"Feeding a dog today means giving them the chance to be someone's joy tomorrow." – Heather Williams

Why we chose this mission.

Feeding dogs isn't a distraction from human need; it's a **direct path into it**. We meet people where they already are—at pantries, schools, community centers—and remove a small, heavy worry that weighs on everything else. The result is quieter homes, fewer surrenders, and communities that feel a little more held.

Small act. Big ripple. A full bowl today, a steadier life tomorrow. It keeps a family together, eases the fear of "what about the dog?" and lowers the chances of a surrender. The care you pour into a pet steadies the humans beside them—calmer evenings, kinder mornings, one less weight to carry. That's how tiny gestures become lasting change.

The Ripple Effect of Compassion

Our work at *Making Change Pawsible* is about more than meals. Every bowl of food delivered is a message—to the dog and their human—that they are not forgotten. Often, these meals go to pets belonging to struggling families, the homeless, or elderly individuals on fixed incomes.

In those moments, feeding a dog feeds more than their stomach—it feeds the human spirit, strengthens the human-animal bond, and eases the burden of those already carrying heavy loads. It buys a night of sleep for a parent choosing between bills and kibble, and it tells a child their best friend is staying home. It gives a senior living alone a reason to get up, move, and say hello to a neighbor. It can be the difference between surrendering a pet to a crowded shelter and keeping the family intact. Small as it seems, a single bag of food creates a ripple of stability—less fear today, more hope tomorrow.

Purpose as a Leadership Lesson

What I've learned is that purpose fuels resilience. The same leadership principles that helped me run healthcare operations— teamwork, resourcefulness, and consistency— also drive this mission. In both worlds, success comes from understanding the needs of those you serve and mobilizing people and resources to meet those needs.

In many ways, *Making Change Pawsible* has been the most rewarding leadership role I've ever had—because every action is deeply personal and every success is shared by the community.

How You Can Make Change Pawsible

You don't have to start a nonprofit to find purpose beyond yourself. You just must take one small step toward helping others. For some, that might be donating to a local shelter. For others, it might be volunteering, fostering, or simply spreading awareness.

Ways to help dogs in need:

1. Donate dog food or supplies to local shelters.

2. Sponsor a dog's meals for a month.

3. Advocate for responsible pet ownership in your community.

    "The meaning of life is to find your gift. The purpose of life is to give it away." — Pablo Picasso

Closing Thought

Finding purpose beyond self rarely arrives as a lightning bolt. More often, it grows in quiet inches—through consistent acts of compassion that no one applauds but everyone feels. For me, that purpose has four legs, a wagging tail, and a mission that won't let go: **make sure no dog goes hungry**.

Purpose shifts the scoreboard. You stop measuring life only by promotions and start measuring it by the peace you leave in a home, the relief in a caregiver's eyes, the stillness of a pup that goes to sleep with a full belly. It's not grand; it's faithful. And faithfulness, repeated, becomes significance.

If you're searching for your "bigger than me," start small. Do for one what you wish you could do for many. Feed one bowl. Make one call. Host one drive. The path to significance is paved with ordinary steps taken on purpose.

"When you find the cause that speaks to your soul, you stop chasing success—and start living significance." – Heather Williams

Final Chapter – Living M·I·M·E Every Day

Living M·I·M·E isn't a one-time breakthrough. It's a rhythm. It's the drumbeat you keep when the music changes, the steady cadence that turns ordinary days into a life you're proud of. If this book sounds repetitive, that's because my life has been repetitive—on purpose. The same small, deliberate actions— done repeatedly—built my results, repaired my relationships, and clarified my purpose. Repetition wasn't a rut; it was the road.

At McDonald's, repetition looked like temp checks, clean-as-you-go, drive-thru timing, and ten-minute huddles. In healthcare, it was identity verification, warm transfers, note hygiene, and daily coaching. In community service, it's pet pantry pop-ups, follow-ups, and the promise to show up next month, too. The wins didn't come from occasional heroics; they came from consistent habits— reps that taught my mind and my team what "good" feels like until it became who we were.

"Consistency isn't boring—it's compounding." – Heather Williams

Why Repetition Works

- **Reps beat willpower.** When something becomes a habit, you don't fight yourself to do it—you just do it.

- **Reps create reliability.** People trust what you do consistently, not what you promise occasionally.

- **Reps compound.** One percent better today becomes unmistakable progress by season's end.

- **Reps reveal reality.** When you repeat a process, patterns—and opportunities to improve—become obvious.

The M·I·M·E Loop (Your Daily Engine)

M·I·M·E—**Mindset, I'm Possible, Mediocrity, Extraordinary**—isn't just a framework; it's a loop you can run every day:

1. **Mindset (Set your lens)**

   Choose how you'll see the day. Ask: *What's the most useful lens? What's the first inch?*

2. **I'm Possible (Choose a stretch)** Name one small action that moves a hard thing forward. *Not everything—just the next step.*

3. **Mediocrity (Embrace the plateau)** Expect the "ordinary" phase. Use it to refine fundamentals, not to judge yourself.

4. **Extraordinary (Lift by 1%)**

   Raise the floor: tighten one step, clean one handoff, show one extra ounce of care.

Then repeat tomorrow. That repetition—*with reflection*—is how average becomes excellent.

"Live M·I·M·E and let your reps speak louder than your doubts." - Heather Williams

A Simple M·I·M·E Practice

Morning (5 minutes):

- *Mindset:* Write one sentence about how you'll show up.
- *I'm Possible:* Pick one stretch action for the day.

Midday (2 minutes):

- *Mediocrity:* Where did things feel "meh"? Note one tiny fix.

Evening (5 minutes):

- *Extraordinary:* Capture one win you created by doing the basics well. Set tomorrow's first inch.

Weekly and Monthly Reps

Weekly (15 minutes):

- Keep / Tweak / Toss one micro- process.
- Share one specific win and one next behavior with your team or family.

Monthly (30 minutes):

- Re-anchor priorities (work + home).
- Add or retire one ritual.
- Ask, *Where did repetition pay off? Where did it drift?*

What "Living M·I·M·E" Looks Like
in Real Life

- **Work:** Open with clarity, close the loop, coach one behavior a week, and let your metrics reflect care—not just speed.
- **Home:** Red-letter calendar, device- free dinners, weekly walks, and one tradition that sticks.
- **Purpose:** One pop-up, one follow-up, one family kept together because a bowl was full.

Repetition built my career, restored my balance, and revealed my purpose. The same ordinary actions—done on purpose, again tomorrow—turned setbacks into systems and systems into significance.

"Believe—then behave like you believe. Your reps will carry you where motivation can't." – Heather Williams

Closing Thought

If you remember nothing else, remember this: **You must live a life M·I·M·E.** Choose your **Mindset**. Declare **I'm Possible**. Treat **Mediocrity** as a training ground. Deliver the **Extraordinary** by raising the floor one inch at a time. Do it today. Do it again tomorrow. Let the repetition become your proof.

Because success and fulfillment aren't built by what you do *once*— they're built by how you **show up every day**.

M – Mindset

Mindset is the foundation. Every day presents a choice—to react or to respond, to complain or to create solutions, to shrink from challenges or rise to them. Your mindset doesn't just shape your day; it shapes your future. Build it on purpose: audit your self-talk ("How can I?" instead of "I can't"), set a first- minute ritual that centers you, and surround yourself with people who expect growth.

I – I'm Possible

The difference between "impossible" and "I'm possible" is belief backed by action. You will face doubters. You will face moments where you don't feel ready. That's where this principle matters most. Start before you feel prepared—take one small step, learn quickly, and stack wins. Let preparation be your proof: do the research, build the checklist, ask for feedback, then move. Courage isn't the absence of fear; it's momentum despite it, turning "not yet" into "now."

M – Mediocrity (as a Steppingstone)

Mediocrity is not a verdict—it's a stage. It's the place where you gain skills, discipline, and clarity before making the leap to greatness. Use it as a training ground: master fundamentals, tighten one habit a week, and treat every plateau as data, not defeat. Ask, "What more can I do?" and then pull one small lever you can measure. With patience and repetition, that "middle" becomes momentum—and momentum becomes mastery.

E – Extraordinary

Extraordinary is found in the ordinary—how you handle small tasks, how you treat people, how you show up when no one is watching. Excellence in the little things paves the way for excellence in the big things. When you pre-stage what's needed, leave clean notes, and close the loop without being asked, those micro-choices compound into trust. Ordinary moments shape your character—and your culture—long before the spotlight arrives.

Keep doing the ordinary on purpose, and one day people will call it extraordinary.

Beyond the Acronym: The Life it Builds.

Living *M·I·M·E* is about more than professional success. It's about becoming the kind of leader, parent, friend, and citizen who leaves people, places, and causes better than you found them.

For me, it meant finding purpose in *Making Change Pawsible*, feeding dogs who can't feed themselves, and reclaiming a personal life that had been sacrificed for years in the name of a career. It meant understanding that leadership isn't about being the most

knowledgeable person in the room—it's about influencing, empowering, and inspiring others to reach their best.

Your Invitation

Now it's your turn.

You've walked the floors with me—from lunch rushes to patient calls, from sacrifice to service. But reading *about* M·I·M·E is only the first step. **Living it** is where transformation happens—quietly at first, then unmistakably.

Ask yourself each day:

- Am I protecting my **Mindset**?
- Am I acting like **I'm Possible** today?
- Am I moving beyond **Mediocrity** (one inch at a time)?
- Am I finding the **Extraordinary** in the ordinary?

"The real measure of success is not in the titles you earn or the money you make—it's in the lives you impact, including your own."
– Heather Williams

The Four Commitments (M·I·M·E in motion)

1. **Mindset:** I will choose a useful lens before I act.

2. **I'm Possible:** I will take one small step toward a big thing, every day.

3. **Mediocrity (as a stage):** I will treat plateaus as practice fields, not verdicts.

4. **Extraordinary:** I will raise the floor— make the worst day better— by 1%.

A 7-Day Jumpstart

- **Day 1 – Mindset:** Write one sentence about how you'll show up. Put it where you'll see it.

- **Day 2 – I'm Possible:** Tackle a 15-

  minute action you've been postponing.

- **Day 3 – Mediocrity:** Name one "meh"

  process. Improve one step.

- **Day 4 – Extraordinary:** Deliver an ordinary task with uncommon care. Notice the ripple.

- **Day 5 – Relationship:** Encourage one person—specific praise, one ask to help them grow.

- **Day 6 – Service:** Do one small act for someone (or some-pup) who can't pay you back.

- **Day 7 – Reflect:** Capture three lessons, one habit to keep next week.

The 30-Day "One-Inch" Sprint

- **Weekly focus:**
  - Week 1: **Preparation** (checklists, staging, quick answers)
  - Week 2: **Communication**

    (clarity, tone, warm handoffs)
  - Week 3: **Handoffs** (clean notes, closed loops, kept promises)
  - Week 4: **Consistency** (daily rhythm, first-5 / last-5, tiny audits)
- **Rule:** One inch a day. Measure one number. Celebrate one win. Repeat.

Your Accountability Map

- **Name a witness:** Tell one person your

  next step and when you'll do it.
- **Red-letter your life:** Put the people and practices that matter **on your calendar first**.
- **Pick your practice:** First 20 / Last 20 (no email), device-free dinners, weekly walk.
- **Leave a trail:** Journal two lines a day—what you moved, what you learned.

From Success to Significance

Goals are good. **Meaning is better.** As you live M·I·M·E, aim your growth beyond yourself:

- Mentor one person for 30 days.

- Support a small local mission—or start a micro-one of your own.

- If dogs are part of your heart, feed one bowl, host one mini-drive, or share **Making Change Pawsible** with someone who needs it.

The M·I·M·E Pledge

I will choose my mindset.

I will act like I'm possible.

I will treat mediocrity as a training ground, not a label.

I will do the ordinary with extraordinary care—again tomorrow.

Pin it. Post it. Live it.

You don't need a perfect plan. You need a

first step—today.

When you commit to living M·I·M·E, you aren't just chasing goals; you're building a life that quietly invites others to believe in what's possible for themselves. That is the legacy worth leaving.

The page turns to you now. **Begin.**

References

Buckingham, M. (2007). *Go Put Your Strengths to Work*. Free Press.

Buckingham, M., & Goodall, A. (2019). *Nine Lies About Work*. Harvard Business Review Press.

Buckingham, M. (2022). *Love + Work*. Harvard Business Review Press.

Centers for Medicare & Medicaid Services. (n.d.). *Patient experience and quality measures*. https://www.cms.gov

Covey, S. R. (1989). *The 7 habits of highly effective people*. Simon & Schuster.

Dweck, C. S. (2006). *Mindset: The new psychology of success*. Random House.

Gallup Workplace Research. (n.d.).

Employee engagement and leadership effectiveness. https://www.gallup.com

Greenleaf, R. K. (1977). *Servant*

leadership: A journey into the nature of legitimate power and greatness. Paulist Press.

Harvard Business Review. (n.d.).

Leadership, influence, and resilience in organizational environments.

https://hbr.org

Hepburn, A. (n.d.). *Nothing is impossible. The word itself says, 'I'm possible.'* [Quote].

Maxwell, J. C. (2007). *The 21 irrefutable laws of leadership.* Thomas Nelson.

McDonald's Corporation. (n.d.). *Under the Arches Program.* McDonald's.

Sinek, S. (2009). *Start with why: How great leaders inspire everyone to take action.* Portfolio

www.ingramcontent.com/pod-product-compliance
Lightning Source LLC
LaVergne TN
LVHW041317080426
835513LV00008B/497